Jerry

So glad you have c...
into our lives
Much love
Amy

When God Has a Way,
No Other Way Works

Proverbs
3:5-7
"Trust in the Lord
your heart..."
with all

July 10, 2015

Amy Alford Crafton !

xulon
PRESS

Inspirational! Amy has a simple, yet profound way of sharing. Her compassionate, beautiful spirit brought me to a deeper place in my relationship with God as I turned each page. As Sandy was to Amy, an angel sent from God to bring her closer to Him, Amy now generously passes on what she has learned in a concise, easy to read gem! This book awakened me...her words gently remind us of the things that truly matter in life!

BRIDGET BENENATE
AWARD-WINNING SONGWRITER FOR JACI
VELASQUEZ AND KELLY CLARKSON'S NO. 1
SINGLE, "BREAKAWAY"
LOS ANGELES, CA

Through a very practical, everyday style Amy offers amazing insight and understanding to some of the joys, challenges and temptations that we face on a regular basis. She shares personal life experiences that are easy to relate to and full of the encouragement and hope that you may be needing! Grab a cup of coffee, relax and allow Amy to take you on a journey that may bring a whole new, fulfilling perspective into your daily life!

DR. JOE WHITE
PRESIDENT, KANAKUK KAMPS

Amy's winsome spirit shines through in this very approachable book. As she shares the life lessons that have inspired her faith, you will feel as if you are in an easy conversation with an open, honest soul. Be assured that you will glean practical truths taught by a fellow spiritual sojourner.

DR. LES CARTER
AUTHOR OF *THE ANGER TRAP*

When God gets involved, little things make a huge impact. (Goliath learned this lesson the hard way!) In this warmly personal story, Amy Alford takes us on a journey showing how an ordinary woman named Sandy impacted her life in a big way. Sandy's commitment to the faithful transfer of a lifetime of insights from one generation to the next is an inspiration to follow. I know I was inspired to go and do likewise. I hope you will be, too.

GARY BRANDENBURG
SENIOR PASTOR, FELLOWSHIP DALLAS

I couldn't put it down. It's an excellent tool for new Christians wanting to learn the basics of how to walk by faith in a relationship with Jesus Christ.

JOHN MAISEL
FOUNDER AND PRESIDENT OF EAST WEST MINISTRIES INTERNATIONAL

Sandy, thank you for all the days and time you spent with me. I'm so blessed to have you in my life to encourage, support, and inspire me. Your knowledge and wisdom of our Lord has overflowed not only to me, but to those who are fortunate enough to know you. You are a glowing illustration of one who walks the walk. Thanks for loving me and sharing with me all these years.

Table of Contents

About the Author.. xiii

Introduction... xvii

Chapter 1 Beginning Again.................................... 19

Chapter 2 Dealing with Pain................................. 33

Chapter 3 Growing in Christ................................. 49

Chapter 4 God Has a Plan..................................... 71

Chapter 5 Knowing and Doing God's Will.......... 97

Chapter 6 Surrendering Control........................... 117

Chapter 7 Praying with Power.............................. 133

Chapter 8 Sharing Your Faith............................... 149

Chapter 9 What Is Your Story? 167

Epilogue How to Become a Christian..................... 181

S pecial thanks goes to my mom for taking me to Sandy's Bible class so many years ago and for introducing me to my "adopted grandmother." My mom, step-dad and dad have always been an incredible influence on my life. Thank you all for loving me and caring for me through all the things I've been through. You've always been there for me, and I'm forever thankful. Thanks for being my role models and for teaching me along the way about life. I love you all so very much; you are the best parents anyone could ask for.

To my husband, Ben, thanks for encouraging me to write this book and being my inspiration in life. The Lord blessed me double when He brought me you. Thanks for always being there, for loving me and for letting me "get away" to write this and encouraging me to tell some of my stories. It's been an inspiring journey. I love you, Sweet One. "I could not ask for more."

Special thanks to David Edmonson, Sandy's sweet son, who photographed us for the cover and spent hours in the studio making everything perfect. Luke Edmonson, Sandy's grandson, for being so patient with me while

I try to figure out this crazy computer! Vicky Mullins, Radha Mayo and Denise Gilbert for hours of typing the manuscript from pages of my illegible handwriting. To Mary Ann Lackland for countless hours helping me with the book. I could not have done it without her.

To Susan Pausky for inspiring me and being an example of dedicating the next 25 years of her life to God's service instead of waiting until the last five years. To my sweet friend, Melissa, for sharing with me and allowing me to pray for you during the trials that you endured. I was honored to be alongside you during those times.

Most of all, for all of Sandy's encouraging words and advice that inspired me to write this book.

About the Author

Wife, daughter and friend are just a few of the hats that author, Amy Alford, wears on a daily basis. A professional photographer since 1989, Amy has photographed some of the world's most powerful and respected leaders, including President George Bush, Jr. and his wife Laura, as well as former President George Bush, Sr., Oprah Winfrey, Benjamin Netanyahu, Senator Kay Bailey Hutchinson and Bill Cosby. However, nothing excites her more than capturing the special moments of children and families. She graduated from Brooks Photography Institute in Santa Barbara, California.

Amy has taken several mission trips and has had moving moments in poverty stricken places from Russian orphanages to small villages in Cuba. Amy enjoys her involvement in door-to-door ministry in foreign countries, prison ministry, Bible Study and her involvement in Fellowship Bible Church. Amy is also passionate about capturing God's breathtaking nature with her camera. He creates it, and she captures it.

She and her husband love to travel throughout the world. Her favorite places include her family farms in Ozark, Arkansas and McKinney, Texas, summers in Aspen Colorado and Santa Barbara, California. When she is not behind the camera, she loves adventure-activities like snow skiing, four-wheelers, paragliding, sky diving, bungee jumping and tennis. On the softer side, a beautiful sunset, thunderstorms and a good fire are among Amy's favorite things.

Reaching out to people is one of Amy's spiritual gifts, and Amy has devoted a lot of her time to Christian-based organizations. She serves on the board of "Council for Life," a Christ-centered organization that supports agencies that help women with unplanned pregnancies. Amy gladly donates her time and money to their cause. She also supports "Youth Believing in Change," a ministry to under-privileged kids. Their after-school program teaches kids about the Bible, helps them with homework and gives them a snack while they wait for their parents to get home from work. This organization keeps kids off the streets and away from drugs.

Amy feels strongly about sponsoring short-term mission trips, following Christ's command to "Go into all nations and spread the gospel." She has been on mission trips with East West Ministries, a ministry that focuses on places in the world where less than 1% of the people have heard of Christ. She loves to go with them whenever her schedule permits. She also volunteers at her church in the prayer rooms and is a member of the hospital visitation team. Showing people there is someone who cares, especially in their time of need, is important to her. She and her husband, Ben, reside in Dallas, Texas with their dog, Buddy.

Introduction

S ometimes the best lessons are those you learn from watching someone else "do life." If we pay attention, we can learn life lessons from others all the time. Some people teach us how *not* to live—and what to learn from their mistakes. Yet once in a while God sends someone into our lives who changes us forever. They're the kind of people who influence our lives and teach us important lessons about God and His purpose for our lives. That was what my mentor and "adopted grandmother," Sandy Edmonson, did for me.

This is a true story about our friendship. It's about an unexpected relationship that bound two women from different generations on the same journey in life. One woman was three steps ahead of the other—older and wiser. (I was the other one, younger and not as wise as I thought.) At first, I was simply hoping a little bit of what Sandy had would rub off me. Over time, I realized that God had more in mind. He wanted to use Sandy to bring me closer to Him than ever before.

I didn't know her at all when we began meeting together, but today I couldn't do without her. She started out as a "sounding board" for me when I was going through some difficult times. However, as we got to know each other, I grew to think of her as more of a friend and, eventually, even family. We jokingly call ourselves "adopted" grandmother and granddaughter. We have spent countless hours together over many years, drinking coffee at Starbucks and talking about life.

Sandy has a way of sharing what the Bible says in a realistic and simple way that teaches me about living my life. She simplifies everyday struggles and concerns in a way that is easier to understand. By showing me how verses from the Bible apply to my modern day needs and struggles, she has helped and encouraged me so much. Listening to her helpful suggestions (that I believe were prompted by the Lord) has strengthened my faith.

They say every relationship changes a person. I believe that's true because as I grew in my relationship with the Lord, he began to heal my hurts and unveil good things in me as well. He revealed a sense of compassion and hope among layers of giving and caring in my soul that I never knew existed. That miracle of transformation is what this story is about.

God is at work to change all of us into the image of His Son. It happens all the time, I know. However, I have to believe that our story is unique. God brought Sandy into my life in order to help me become the person I never knew I could be. Through sharing this story, I hope I can pass on to you what the Lord taught me through our friendship. Who knows? God may have someone unexpected in mind for you to pass on these same, simple truths.

Chapter 1

Beginning Again

My dad was dying of cancer, my marriage had fallen apart, I had just moved back home to Dallas to take care of my dad and I had started my own photography business. When Sandy and I first began getting to know one another, life was messy. I was not too proud to admit that I was having a hard time holding it all together. I needed spiritual guidance, and I needed it quickly.

Sandy Edmonson became my spiritual mentor and friend in a very short time despite the 45-year age difference between us. She was born before World War II, the greatest generation as they say. I was born in the sixties, when "anything goes" was the new motto and bell bottoms were in. I was starting over in my early thirties, and Sandy was looking back on the horizon of a successful life as a wife, mother and now grandmother and great-grandmother. We came from two completely different worlds, but none of that seemed to matter at the time.

I can see that the Lord put Sandy in my life at just the right time and at just the right place. He used her to show me God's compassion and love for those who are suffering through difficult times. Step by step, He also used her to help me get back on track with my relationship with Him.

Meeting Sandy for the First Time

Shortly after I moved home to Dallas in the fall of 1991, Mom invited me to go with her to Sandy's Bible study—a class that she had been teaching for the past 27 years. I wasn't so sure that I wanted to do that. I didn't know who Sandy was, but I knew I'd already spent too much time alone feeling sad about my marriage and my father, so I agreed. When we walked in, Sandy glanced up and she offered a glowing, contagious smile. She looked so happy to see my mom and me as mom introduced us and her warmth welcomed me into the room.

I didn't remember meeting Sandy before, but to my surprise she said that she remembered me from the time I was three years old. It turns out that the Bible class was held in the same church I had attended when I was a child. Sandy recalled seeing me sitting in front of her with my parents. One Sunday, my dad turned his head to whisper to me and Sandy noticed his dark, long eyelashes. She thought to herself, "I hope their little girl has those eyelashes!" Ironically, here was that little girl thirty years later in the same church attending Bible class with Sandy.

Much later after we got to know each other, Sandy told me about a funny discovery she had made. She said, "I was cleaning out a closet and found this old church directory. It's funny, but our pictures are right next to one another." When I opened the book and saw our pictures I smiled and said, "Oh, Sandy, we have to put this photo in my book!"

She looked rather concerned and exclaimed, "Honey, my hair is so big!" "Don't worry," I told her, "so was Mom's!"

Settling into a nearby comfortable chair, I did not know exactly what to expect from the Bible study. To my surprise, I soon found myself scrambling for pen and paper to write down some of the things I was hearing. Sandy's words caught my attention, and her message intrigued me. I had heard the Gospel many times before and had been a Christian since I was a child. However, at this time in my life, my heart was so open, and I was ready to listen to whatever God wanted me to know. The Holy Spirit made my eyes and ears willing to see and hear what the Bible had to say through the words that Sandy spoke. What she taught me about God that day and for several months and years after that made me want to know Him on a deeper level. As my friendship with Sandy deepened, so did my relationship with God.

Going through Changes

With all the changes I was going through, sometimes I was so down and upset that I didn't know what to do or even what to feel. Mom has always been the one I turned to first, but even Mom didn't have all the answers. That's when she would say, "Honey, do you want me to call Sandy and see if she has time to see you?" Sandy always made time for me, even in the beginning when she hardly knew me.

I remember driving to Sandy's house to talk with her one-on-one for the first time. I had been attending the Bible study class for a while, but I had never told her about my life and what I was going through. I was thinking, "How can she make me feel better?" I was so far down in the dumps that all I wanted to do was hit a hundred tennis balls as hard as I could. Anger and frustration, combined with a sense of helplessness, had overtaken my mind, body and soul. How could Sandy help me out of that?

Sandy greeted me at the door and welcomed me inside. There was a staircase to the right of the front door. As I looked up the stairs, I wondered what her children's rooms were like. Her husband Red had passed away several years before, and all her children were grown and living in their own homes by now.

Quietly, I followed her around the corner to her study. Soft light from a lamp on the desk glowed dimly, but most of the light shown through the window blinds. I sat down on a yellow love seat facing her. She sat next to the window near a bookcase full of books.

As we began to talk about what was bothering me at the time, she never took her eyes off me. There was something warm and comforting about her presence that drew me to share things I had never shared with anyone else. The upheaval in my life seemed such a contrast to her as she patiently listened to my struggles. As I poured out my story in starts and stops, her steady but kind gaze began to unnerve me. I found myself looking around the room and avoiding eye contact while we talked on.

At one point, she reached over to the bookcase and grabbed a well-worn Bible. (You know what they say: "A Bible that is torn up and frayed usually means the owner is not.") She began reading some verses that paralleled some of what she was telling me. What she said never sounded preachy or as if she were talking down to me. In fact, she didn't speak on her own authority, as though she was the expert. She gently made suggestions and explained how the Lord desires us to come to Him with our troubles.

During that first day in Sandy's home, it seemed as though the world had grown quiet and all I heard was Sandy's sweet, understanding and attentive voice. As I look back on that day, I realize it was the Holy Spirit whispering to my heart, bringing a warm, gentle feeling of peace and calm over me.

Gaining a New Perspective

With every Scripture that Sandy read to me that day, it was as if someone peeled off another layer of despair surrounding my body. If it had not happened to me, I wouldn't have believed the healing effect of simply listening to God's Word. Within an hour's time, I felt as though I were a new person. It seemed as if the anguish and despair fell to the floor—a thousand pounds had been lifted off my shoulders. Where those heavy feelings of oppression went, I still don't know. Sure, I had many days of sadness and uncertainty ahead of me, but now I also had hope.

As I told Sandy what was going on in my life, she picked Scriptures for me that pertained to my specific problem. This became the pattern of our meetings together. She knew the Bible so well. The Bible says to "pray without ceasing." In other words, be "God conscious" and communicate with Him all day long. I felt as though the Lord was speaking straight through Sandy to my heart.

She taught me that the Bible says that He will bring us peace if we give ourselves, our problems and our sufferings to Him in the midst of trials. That is exactly what happened to me on those afternoons I spent with Sandy.

I knew that I hadn't gotten very far carrying them all by myself. I had exhausted myself physically, emotionally and spiritually trying to resolve my problems and circumstances all alone. I was going about it all wrong—covering up the issues, ignoring them or doing quick-fixes that never really solved anything.

I could try to fix things all day long, but only when I said, "Okay, Lord, I give up. I need your help. I can't do it on my own," did the Lord move in and take over. I was still struggling to get my life together and begin a new business. I desperately wanted to get past this stage! Sandy met my impatience head on and reminded me that God would not necessarily take me *out* of my circumstances. She said that He would bring me peace and give me strength to *endure* what He had allowed me to experience. Each trial and difficult circumstance we endure strengthens our faith. We learn valuable lessons that draw us closer to the Lord—which is exactly what He wants.

Sandy and I eventually started meeting at Starbucks, quite the social scene! Sometimes we went to our favorite cafeteria for our talks. We liked it there because nobody rushed us to leave or interrupted our conversation. Time sort of stopped, just for us it seemed. As she talked, I was so struck by her wisdom that I inevitably began scribbling notes on napkins, receipts and any scrap paper in my purse. Each time we met, which was two or three times every month, I realized more and more that God had been at work in my life for a long time.

Growing up in a Godly Family

My parents became Christians when I was a child and provided a solid foundation for my faith. I remember the change in the household after they became believers. We would sit together on the floor in the living room and Dad would read devotionals to us. My older brother, Andy, and I learned about Jesus early on, thank goodness. When I was nine years old we were living in Dallas, Texas, and I attended a nearby Christian camp called "Pine Cove" with Andy. This is where I accepted Christ as my Savior.

I remember that my camp counselor and I walked down to the beautiful lake one afternoon and talked about Jesus. When we reached the bank of the water, we got down on our knees and made an "ichthus" (a Christian symbol that looks like a fish) out of the East Texas red clay. "Muffin"—my counselor's "camp name"—was with me that sunny day at camp when I received Jesus into my life. (Interestingly, I was at Kanakuk, another camp, when I rededicated my life to Christ at the age of 16.) I brought my ichthus home with me because it reminded me of my decision to follow Christ. I will never forget the look on my parents' faces when I told them I had become a Christian.

My dad was a great dad. Andy and I were the apple of his eye. To me, he was the picture- perfect father. He spent lots of time with me, teaching me how to play every sport imaginable. He was so patient with me and wanted me to have fun everywhere I went. When most of my friends were just getting their training wheels off, Dad and I spent hours in the driveway learning to ride that one-wheel bike, the unicycle. I always challenged myself no matter what I was doing. Mom and Dad were right there beside me encouraging me and supporting me.

People say I look most like my mom, who is such a godly woman. I'd love to grow up and be just like her. She handles everything so well and always has great advice. She never gets flustered or stressed, and she is so nice to everyone. Her godliness shows in her attitude, and that's why she has so many friends. When we get together, we have fun no matter what and often laugh until our stomachs hurt. I'm glad I had the kind of mom I did when I was growing up, but I'm even more thankful for the relationship we have now. It's great to have your mom be your best friend!

As a child, I was not the best student. My grades weren't great and I always seemed to be getting into trouble. I was very adventuresome and, at times, even rebellious. I am sure it was a full-time job raising me. I was the "wild child," but my older brother, Andy, on the other hand, was the "good child." I kept my parents on their toes, but I relished the fact that I always had a good time.

I got my first job when I was only 13—dipping cones at Swenson's ice cream shop. In eighth grade, I wanted to get a job at Kip's Big Boy. I was only 14 at the time, and you had to be 16 to work there, but I had my mind set on earning money and saving enough to buy a car. I remember spilling coffee once on a customer and accidentally flipping a dirty fork onto someone's lap! However, I worked hard, and I enjoyed working with people. When I was in high school, I got a job at a restaurant near my high school helping the chef in the kitchen. I was pretty good at making 12-egg omelettes (once I learned to crack eggs with both hands simultaneously!). I liked the fact that the restaurant was near school so that when I got off work I could run by the football game and get together with my friends.

One summer, I worked at my step-father's flight school. I pictured me washing airplanes in my bikini and working on my tan. Was I surprised when I landed in the front office instead, answering phones and filing papers.

After graduating from high school in Dallas, I decided to attend the University of Arkansas. I had a growing interest in photography, always carrying around a camera with me in high school and early college. However, I didn't know that you could actually make a living taking photographs. Whenever I took my camera with me, my friends would always moan and say, "Stop taking our pictures!" But they were also the first ones to ask me for a copy later.

I took my first photography class my freshman year in college. I remember developing my first photograph one day in the dark room. In that moment, I realized that I wanted to be a photographer more than anything in the world. I was fascinated as I watched a blank image transform into a clean, crisp photo before my eyes. I was hooked. I ran to my professor and said, "This is what I want to do for the rest of my life!"

My professor recommended that I look into transferring to Brooks Institute in Santa Barbara, California. I wasn't even sure where that was, but I contacted them and sent for a catalog. When I opened the catalog, I was so excited because of the beautiful pictures of the Santa Barbara beach! Even though it was hundreds of miles away, I was always prone to adventure and looked forward to a new challenge. After getting some of my basic college classes out of the way at the University of Arkansas, I transferred to Brooks and began learning about the world of photography.

Moving Cross Country

Two years after I moved to Santa Barbara, and a lot of film, cameras and tripods later, my high school boyfriend moved out. We had dated throughout college, and we married the year I graduated from Brooks. We decided to stay in California for a while, but after four months of crime and earthquakes, we had had enough of the coast. He was a hotel chef in Beverly Hills and I was a budding photographer, which meant we were lucky enough to live almost anywhere and be able to find jobs. One day we decided to move to the island of Maui because he could get a job with another hotel there.

I got a job as a waitress in the restaurant on the ground floor of the condo where we lived. It was great—if I had to be at work at five, I could leave at five and still be there on time! One day I noticed an ad in the paper for a photography company. I called about the ad and was one of 15 people interviewing for the job. Although I was young and fresh out of school, I got the job.

Soon, I was helping shoot beautiful Hawaiian weddings, fun Luaus on the beach and even took part behind the scenes at the Iron Man Marathon. My company made a huge slide show presentation at the end of the race, and I was thrilled to take part in such a famous event. I was learning the ropes of a professional photography business and enjoying it.

Two years later, we decided to try the mountains for a change. We moved to Aspen, Colorado—a truly incredible, beautiful place. It was a town I was familiar with since my family had been going there since I was fourteen. It was like a second home to me (and still is). By this time, I had learned so much about the photography business from my time in Maui. I felt confident enough starting my own business and even placed an ad in the yellow pages. I began slowly, which gave me time to fine-tune my skills and still take time to enjoy the mountains!

However, not everything was as glamorous as it might seem on the surface. It's not easy to start your own business. Between my occasional photo shoots, I worked another job in a restaurant/bar, checking coats in order to make ends meet. My marriage also began unraveling during that time. Looking back, I think living in a gorgeous place made it easier to ignore or cover up any struggles I was having.

Devastating News

One day the phone rang and everything in my world came crashing down around me. My father was sick. Really sick. He had been diagnosed with cancer five years earlier and survived. Now it had returned and the outcome did not look good.

Although my parents had divorced when I was 12 years old, they remained friends and I grew close to both of them as I grew into adulthood. My father and I always had a special bond. I remember we would go places together in the car when I was a child, laughing and enjoying just being together.

Many times he would let me steer, even though I wasn't old enough to drive. One of our favorite songs to sing together when it came on the radio was, "You Are the Sunshine of My Life." We declared it to be "our song." He would often sing the first part of the chorus, "You are the sunshine of my life...," to which I would respond, "You are the apple of my eye." The song summed up the special way we felt about each other. One day when I was in grade school, I made a hook rug pillow of an apple for a class project and proudly gave it to him. He displayed my little pillow front and center on his sofa until he died. I always think of him to this day whenever I look at it or hear that song.

Needless to say, I was terrified that Dad was sick again and might even die, and I could hardly stand to think about it. I had a sinking feeling in my stomach as I hung up the phone that day, but I picked it up again immediately and began making arrangements to fly home as soon as possible.

"Come near to God and he will come near to you."
James 4:8

"Cast all your anxiety on him because he cares for you."
1 Peter 5:7

Chapter 2

Dealing with Pain

Dad was diagnosed with colon cancer at the age of 50. He ended up having a colostomy. If you are not familiar with that term, don't worry. I wasn't either. Depending on the severity of the disease, one of the ways doctors fight the cancer is by removing a portion of the colon, which is what they did to my dad. Until the body heals and doctors can surgically re-connect the colon, the patient has to wear a bag on his or her waist-line (where bodily waste collects).

Dad never complained about the inconvenience of having "the bag." As a matter of fact, he tried to spare me from any details or visuals because he didn't want me to worry. When we were in the hospital after doctors had given him the bag, my older brother Andy was trying to ease the seriousness of the situation. So, he told us a joke. He said, "Why can't high-society women have a colostomy? Because they can't find shoes to match their bag!" Luckily, Dad had a sense of humor even in a time of sadness. We all had a brief laugh to break the awkwardness of our intense afternoon. After several months with "the bag," Dad had reconstructive surgery to have the bag removed. All went well and he was cancer free. For the time being.

Now, five years later, things had changed. It started when Dad noticed he just wasn't feeling right. When he went to the doctor in 1989, he learned that the cancer was back, this time to stay. I spent the next year flying back and forth between Aspen and Dallas taking care of my dad and going with him to his doctor appointments.

I wanted to be near Dad, but if you have ever flown to and/or from Aspen, you know it's no picnic. The Rocky Mountains are beautiful to look at, but not to fly over in a small plane during a snowstorm. (There were bags of a different kind being used on those flights!) After going back and forth between Colorado and Texas most weekends, my former husband and I finally moved to Dallas so I could be closer to my dad. He had good and bad days, but he didn't seem to be getting better.

Exploratory Surgery

The doctor told my dad that the cancer had come back and it was in his organs. The MRI and CAT scans showed the liver was clear, but most everything else was spotted with cancer. The doctor suggested performing "exploratory surgery" to remove the organs that had cancer, but also to see clearly what was going on inside his body. Dad didn't want to do it.

My brother and I talked to Dad for weeks trying to convince him to do the exploratory surgery. "Dad," I remember saying many times, "we need to see what's going on inside you." I think he was scared to know what was happening inside his body. However, he finally agreed to the surgery and we set the date—with one request. Dad told the doctors, "Do not remove anything unless it's really bad." He had accepted the fact that chemotherapy and radiation would be part of his life soon after the surgery. But he was concerned about removing vital organs.

I don't think I'll ever forget the day of his surgery. After what seemed like an eternity, the doctor called the family into a little room connected to the waiting area lobby. Andy and his wife, Kammy, stood beside me along with Dad's brother, Lindsay, his wife, Iva and their daughter, Jill. We were anxious to hear what the doctor had to say. Still in his scrubs, he leaned back in his chair and casually laced his fingers together. "Well," he began, "I have good news and bad news. What do you want to hear first?"

We quickly decided we wanted to hear the good news first because when Dad went into surgery, there was no good news about it. The doctor said, "The good news is that there was no cancer in his organs. The bad news is that his liver is solid cancer." Simultaneously, everyone exhaled, and the tears started to flow. I didn't know much about the dreaded disease, but I did know that once it is in the liver, you only have a short time to live. There is nothing they can do about it.

Someone asked the doctor, "Is there anything we can do from here on? Are there certain foods he should be eating?" We were looking for some bit of hope. However, the doctor said matter-of-factly, "No...we can't believe the guy is still walking around. We did remove one of his kidneys. It was the size of an NBA basketball." (A healthy kidney should be the size of a small potato.) Then he went on to say, "Let him eat anything he wants and do anything he feels up to doing because he doesn't have long at all."

Stunned, we all left the little room, our heads hanging low. As soon as we reached the waiting area, we turned to one another in a big circle, locked arms and cried out loud, disturbing the entire room. That was just the beginning of many tears to come. Over the next five or six months, the doctors kept finding more and more cancer. It was popping up everywhere in his body. That's when we moved from Aspen in the fall of 1991 to Dallas so I could be with Dad and help him get to the doctor's appointments, radiation and chemo treatments. The radiation and chemo would not help the liver, but hopefully it would help the other cancer the doctors had discovered. Even though my dad was sick, we spent time together, fixing up my house in Dallas. During the day, he helped me on projects like scraping paint off the windows and even helped me make a dark room for my photography in the attic!

Dad Gets a Brain Tumor

Dad had cancer in his lymph nodes (which basically means all over), but the biggest blow came when we took him in for a doctor's visit because he was losing his balance. It was then that they discovered a golf ball-sized brain tumor in the worst place possible. The doctor told us to go home, pack a bag and come right back for surgery scheduled the following day.

I remember walking into Mom's bedroom that afternoon. She was on the phone, so I sat quietly in front of her at her desk and waited. When she got off the phone, she could tell something was wrong.

"Honey, what's the matter?" she asked me in a soft voice.

I burst into tears and said, "Now Dad has a brain tumor."

I felt as if the life had been sucked out of me. Between my Dad's illness, problems in my marriage and the stress of starting my photography business in Dallas, I was totally drained.

The next day I went with Andy, Uncle Lindsay, Aunt Iva and Jill to the hospital for Dad's brain surgery. We were all in the room with Dad when two doctors came in, carrying clipboards and wearing white coats. They greeted us and said, "Mr. Fleck, after looking at your x-rays again, it seems to be much more serious than we had anticipated. We would like to give you about 20-30 minutes so you can write your will. We'll be back shortly." We were in shock, again.

During his brain surgery, Andy and I met with several men from Dad's church to pray at the hospital chapel. We all prayed for a long time. There is something moving about a group of people praying aloud in a public place. It's as if you can feel the presence of God. Boy, did I need to feel it that day! I wasn't ready for Dad to leave us, but then again, when is anyone ready to lose someone they love and care for so dearly?

I believe God answered our prayers because Dad came through the surgery great. He even got out of ICU a day earlier than expected. At that point, Andy and I agreed to set out on a mission. Our goal was to persuade Dad to move out of his house in Carrollton (which was easily a half-hour drive away from the nearest hospital) and into an assisted living facility. There he would be closer to the hospital and closer to us. He could live in one of the private apartments on the third floor. In case he needed anything, he only had to push a button for a nurse.

Dad fought the decision, as we thought he might. On some days I felt like the parent, and he was the child. I explained to him why it was best for him to move. However, I think in the back of his mind he didn't want to leave his house because he knew he would never return. He eventually saw the need to be closer to his doctors and his children, and we moved him into the assisted living facility. Mom helped us decorate it so that it looked more like "home" when he first arrived. Instead of going home, I spent several nights there with Dad, curled up on the sofa, just to be close to him.

Times with Dad

Before he moved to his apartment, my dad and I spent time together late one evening that would later prove to be so precious to me. We were at my dad's house, sitting at his dining table as he wrote out plans for his funeral service. The light hanging over the table was the only light illuminating our faces. As he finished for the evening, I asked him, "Dad, when you get to heaven, will you give me a sign or something that you're okay?"

He smiled and put his pen down. "Well, Honey," he began, "I don't know if I'll be able to do that. What kind of sign?"

"Oh, I don't know," I said, "maybe play our song on the radio, or do something that only you and I would know about." He knew exactly what song I was talking about—You Are the Sunshine of My Life.

"Okay, Sweetie," he assured me. "If I can, I'll do it." He smiled again to reassure me and said, "Let's get to bed. It's getting late."

That was one of the few final requests I made of my dad. Prior to my last birthday when he was alive, he asked me what I would like to have as a present. At first I told him not to worry about that—but that was so like him to think of me even when he was hurting. Finally, after he insisted on giving me something, I told him that I would like to have a set of monogrammed notepads. He smiled just as he did that night in the dining room, not saying much about it, but not having to. His smile said enough.

Rushing to the ER

Not two weeks after he moved into the apartment, I got the call from Andy. "Can you go over to Dad's and check on him?" he asked. "I don't think he's doing well."

I got there as fast as I could. Iva and Lindsay where already there, helping him get dressed. I knew he was in horrible pain by the way he looked and acted. I sat beside him on his bed and gently stroked his back.

At this, he winced and said, "Honey, don't...that hurts." I looked down at his feet and they were so swollen that they didn't look like his. A waive of excruciating sadness came over me. The tears began dripping onto my jeans, and I slowly got up with my head down so no one could see my face. I walked into the other room and sat as far away from the bedroom door as possible so he couldn't hear me cry.

The tears flowed with the force of a fire hydrant, and my throat felt as if it was closing up. I was trying with all of my might not to lose it, struggling to get hold of myself. Several minutes passed and Dad walked slowly into the living room where I was.

I wiped my eyes and said as positively as I could, "You ready?"

"Yeah," he managed to say weakly. "Let's go."

We all walked to the elevator, got into Uncle Lindsay's car and drove to the hospital. There was no doubt in my mind that Dad would not be coming back home. As we entered the emergency room at the Presbyterian Hospital, they could tell right away he was extremely sick and offered him a wheelchair (which he gladly accepted). Even though I was only in my late twenties, I took over, operating out of survival mode at that point. I know now it was the Holy Spirit who took over and allowed me to carry on. I wheeled him quickly to the check-in desk at the entrance to the ER. The top of the counter was two feet taller than Dad as he sat in the wheelchair, so I leaned over the counter and answered all of their questions.

I told the people at the front desk that he had severe pain and that he was spitting up blood. I knew that if someone was spitting up blood, something was *really* wrong. In the back of my mind, I knew this was it. God wanted Dad to come home, and I knew it was just a matter of time. It seemed to take forever as they entered the information into the computer, but when I looked down at Dad, he was just sitting patiently. He held out his hand and I gently slipped my hand in his. He looked up at me and said, "I love you, Amy." I bent over and whispered in his ear, "I love you too, Dad...very much." Several thoughts flashed through my mind at that instant as I realized that he would never set foot in my house again...he would never meet the children I hoped to have one day. It took all my strength not to completely fall apart at the counter. I knew I was in charge now, and I had to pull it together until Andy got there.

My Last Night with Dad

Thankfully, they admitted Dad only minutes after we checked in, putting him in a room just out of the hectic traffic flow of the ER. I was so thankful when Andy arrived shortly after that. Andy was my strength, my stronghold, my everything at this point. Quickly, I caught Andy up on what had happened. Dad was continuing to spit up blood, and I was nearly panicking. By this point, Dad was on a stretcher with a metal pan beside him that the nurse had given him to spit in. "My dad is dying," I thought to myself as if to make that fact sink in. "This is the beginning of the end, the very end."

My mind raced through a million thoughts, but all I could manage to pray was, *"God, please help him."* He was in so much pain that he seemed incoherent. I assured him over and over how much I loved him and said, "The Lord is going to take care of you." I didn't expect him to respond, so I was surprised when he replied back to me, "I'm in the Lord's hands."

I did not want to leave Dad's side. Once the nurses settled him into a room in the Jackson building, I watched as he slept quietly with the help of some morphine. Once he was asleep, I went home to change and pack a bag to spend the night. I left a note for my husband (at the time) to come to the hospital. He was on the golf course. I returned to Dad's room and sat with him in the dark. There were so many strange machines, needles and noises. It was all so scary to me. I crawled in bed with Dad between all the tubes and wires and held his hand in mine. I tried to fall asleep, but it was impossible with all the nurses coming and going, odd beeping noises and Dad's loud breathing. I realized that I would be more help to him if I got a good night's sleep, so I went home. I had no idea then what was ahead of me.

Letting Go

The next morning was Tuesday, and at the crack of dawn, I was back in the room with Dad. The only time I left his side was to go to the restroom or get something quickly to eat. I had not slept well in weeks, and I was in more pain than I let on. Every time I went to the bathroom, I noticed blood in the toilet. It frightened me, but I never told anyone about it for fear they would stick me in a hospital room of my own, away from Dad.

In those last days, I would have lived off the vending machines around the hospital had it not been for my mom. She began to bring food up to Dad's room for Andy and me. She wouldn't come in out of respect for my dad because she knew he would not want her or anyone else to see him like this.

On the morning of the third day, a nurse that I had become familiar with approached me. "Can I talk to you for a minute?" she asked. I wondered what she wanted to tell me as I followed her into the hospital hallway. She knew I didn't ordinarily leave his room. "Amy," she started with a calm and gentle voice, "I know this will be hard for you to hear, but your father is hanging on for you. You need to tell him to let go. You need to let him know that you will be okay."

She walked away, and I began to cry like I'd never cried before in my life. I couldn't imagine having the strength to tell my sweet dad that I loved and adored, "Go ahead, let go." Andy, my idol and the one I leaned on, came shortly after the nurse left. I took him into the room next door and told him what the nurse had said. I'd never seen Andy cry before, but we sobbed together for what seemed like an hour.

After we gained our composure, Andy looked at me and said, "Well, let's go tell him." We walked back into Dad's room. He was resting peacefully, but he had not responded to us at all that day. We stood on either side of his bed and held hands. I remember stroking Dad's forehead and touching his shoulder. Tears streamed down my face before I could get one word out.

Finally, I drew myself together and said, "Dad, you have been the best dad in the world. I'm so proud of you. Thank you for loving me and being the best to me. Dad, I want you to know that I'm going to be alright. Andy will take care of me, and we are going to be just fine. I want you to let go now. You're going to a much better place, and I will meet you there someday. Don't worry about me. Just let go and stop fighting."

That was the hardest thing I've ever had to do and ever hope to do. He died about three hours after that. I was holding his hand as he slipped away peacefully. It was a weird, surreal feeling to be with someone and then they just stop breathing. I kept waiting for him to take another breath, but he never did. In one instant he was gone and in the presence of the Lord. Dad had very peacefully crossed over to the other side—the better side—heaven. He had been reunited with his parents and other Christian friends who had gone on before. Dad had been in the hospital just two-and-a-half days.

"You Are the Sunshine of My Life"

Before we could call her and tell her, my mother arrived with food for Andy and me because it was lunchtime. When she stepped off the elevator with both arms full of healthy food, she saw Andy and me sitting in the lobby. She had never seen us far from Dad's room, and she seemed surprised to see us there.

"What are ya'll doing out here?" she tentatively asked. Andy looked up and said simply, "It's over." Mom let both sacks of food fall to the floor. The three of us stood in a group hug and cried another round of tears. Even though Mom and Dad had been divorced for years, she mourned him as the father of her children. She had even used some of her personal contacts to help him get the best doctors for his type of cancer. After we made the necessary arrangements and left the hospital, we went to Mom's house for lunch. We prayed and thanked the Lord that Dad did not suffer. We were grateful that he was no longer in any pain or agony and never would be again.

We were sitting on the back porch and Mom had the radio playing in the background. Just as we started to eat our sandwiches I heard, "You Are the Sunshine of My Life" begin to play over the radio. I smiled, looked up toward heaven and said, "Thank you, Lord." I believe that God was communicating to me that Dad was safe in heaven. However, that was only the first of several signs over the coming days that God gave me to assure me. Especially during the week after he died, I felt a sense of peace and comfort, even as I grieved my father's death.

I don't believe in coincidences—I believe everything happens for a reason. However, I do believe there are situations and circumstances that have no other explanation than to say that God did it. The morning of Dad's funeral, I experienced another one. I was getting ready to leave when the doorbell rang. I couldn't imagine who was coming over at a time like this. When I opened the door, I was surprised to see it was a UPS delivery. I opened the little box and inside found a birthday present from my father. He had ordered the monogrammed note cards I wanted for my birthday. (I still have some of the note cards to this day because I can't bear to use the last one.)

After Dad was gone, I was going through some of his "keepsake" boxes of things I had made throughout my childhood—artwork, photos, trinkets and a heavy object wrapped very well in old paper towels. I held it carefully in one hand, while I unraveled it with the other. After a few turns, it fell into my palm. It was the ichthus I had made with the East Texas clay, so many years ago. Unbeknownst to me, he had kept it, securely wrapped and hidden in a safe place.

Another Sign from Dad

My dad had a few idiosyncrasies that I adored, one of which was putting strips of tape on his suitcase. He said it was so he could "identify it easier" at the airport. About six months after he died, I planned a trip to Maui to visit some friends. As I sat in my seat on the plane and watched each person walk by, I noticed an elderly lady coming my way. There was something peaceful about her, and for some reason I found myself thinking, "I wonder if she's an angel?"

I was glad when she ended up sitting next to me. We enjoyed a great conversation during the entire flight. When we arrived in Maui, we walked together to the luggage claim. "Let me get your suitcase," I offered. "What color is it?"

She said, "It's red—one of the hard-case ones."

Two or three hard-cased red bags came around, and as each one passed I looked to her to signal which one was hers. When the last red bag came out, she pointed at it and nodded. I followed the bag down the carousel and as I reached for it, I noticed that it had strips of tape on it. As I returned with her bag, she thanked me. I had to ask her, "Why do you have strips of tape on your suitcase?"

She said with a smile, "So I can identify it easier." I knew right then that the Lord was giving me another sign that my daddy was safe and sound in heaven, watching over me. I never got the lady's name…but, then again, do angels have names?

God's desire for an intimate communion with us is obvious because He has made Himself accessible to us as our Father. The Bible tells us that He wants us to come to Him and tell Him everything. Release it to Him! Don't wait for a tragedy or crisis in your life to start improving your relationship with God. Start now. If you have a strong relationship with Him, it prepares you for anything you might go through in life.

Feeling Connected to Heaven

After Dad died, I felt so connected to heaven. It was as if a part of me was now there, too. Sometimes to comfort myself, I pictured my dad going through "orientation" as he entered heaven. I imagined an angel might point his wing and say, "Mr. Fleck, over here we have the gardens and waterfalls. Over there are the streets of gold, and you saw the pearly gates when you arrived." It always made me smile.

His death was the first stage of a life-changing experience for me. Even though I had lost my dad, I gained so much spiritually in the months and years to come. It was the death of my dad that brought me closer to the Lord. When my world turned upside down I realized, "Life is short; it's time to do some changing." I began to make some adjustments in my life that started me down the path of building a closer relationship with the Lord. In John 12:24, Jesus said, *"I tell you the truth, unless a kernel of wheat falls to the ground and dies, it remains only a single seed. But if it dies, it produces many seeds."* When Dad died, I believe I became the seed that has produced many other seeds. I learned so much about God and my faith through that experience, and I've had many opportunities to share my story and tell the Gospel of Jesus Christ.

"Consider it pure joy, my brothers, whenever you face trials of many kinds, because you know that the testing of your faith develops perseverance."
James 1:2–3

"Blessed is the man who perseveres under trial, because when he has stood the test, he will receive the crown of life that God has promised to those who love him."
James 1:12

Chapter 3

Growing in Christ

When everything was happening with my dad, Sandy prayed for my family. Even though we didn't really begin meeting consistently until after Dad's death, God used her to help me through it afterwards. Sandy even said one time that if such is possible in heaven, one of the exciting things for Dad would be to know about our sweet relationship; it would be a treasure for him.

She patiently showed me that the Bible also gives us the "Three Ts" to teach us God's view of life: it's a Test, a Trust and a Temporary assignment.

A Trial Is a Test

God gives us many "tests" in our lives, many of which we fail miserably. Some, with the help of God, we pass. When the Lord gives us a trial, He is often testing us to see if we are ready for an assignment. In other words, a trial is not all about us. If we look at it as an assignment for His kingdom, then we can often see purpose through our pain.

Trials also test our faith and ability to trust in Him. During most of my younger years, I "tested" my mom. Things she would ask me to do, I wouldn't. Likewise, the things she told me not to do, I would. I was just checking to see if Mom really knew what she was talking about. Well, she did. The times I decided to do what I wanted to do, I usually ended up learning a very important lesson—and earning a handprint on my behind. I vividly recall getting in big trouble one day in the car with my mother. In a stern voice, she turned to me and said, "I am going to wear you to a frazzle when we get home." At that, I burst into tears, crying uncontrollably. Between sniffles and sobs, I asked her, "What's... a... frazzle?" I didn't know then, but I can tell you all about what a frazzle is now.

When I was growing up, I loved to ride my purple Schwinn bike. It was my pride and joy with its flowered banana seat and high-top handlebars. Mom always asked me to be careful and not to ride so fast. One day, I was peddling as fast as I could down the sidewalk near my house. Suddenly, I saw a gaping crack in the cement coming up fast in front of me. I remember thinking to myself, "I wonder what will happen if I go over that crack wriggling my handle bars from side to side?"

Well, "crack" was the key word. I plunged over it, only to make another "crack" of my own—on my forehead! With a trail of blood running down my face, I managed to walk home, screaming the entire way. I must have been somewhat delirious because I rang the doorbell at my own house instead of letting myself in as usual. My dad opened the door and was shocked to find his little girl covered in blood and crying! All I remember was the panic on his face as he began screaming as loud as me!

Mom was out back feeding our herd of kittens when she heard both of us. Dad swooped me up in his outstretched arms, ran to the kitchen and sat me on the sink. Mom came inside in a hurry, always to the rescue. She got a damp cloth, wiped my face off and held the cloth tightly on my forehead.

"Find Andy and get the car. We are going to the hospital!" she announced.

We all piled into Dad's black 1974 Mustang and sped past the sad remains of my prized purple Schwinn. I remember lying in Mom's lap and looking up into three worried faces peering down at me. I could see through the windshield and noticed when Dad ran a red light. I mumbled, "Dad you just ran a red light."

"Honey, it's okay. This is an emergency," he said and sped on. I didn't know what an emergency meant, but I was about to find out.

Mom said, "Let's all start praying," and everyone did. I knew then that what was happening was not good. Thirteen stitches later, I learned a valuable lesson: even though Mom never said "I told you so," I never went over that crack again.

It's the same way with God. In Scripture, He clearly tells us what to do and not to do. When we go against what He asks of us, we fail and sometimes get hurt. We have to start over if we don't learn the lesson. God will send us "around the track" for another lap again and again until we get it. Sometimes we get it the first time around, and sometimes it takes a lifetime before we understand what God is teaching us. That's why it's important to ask God to open your eyes so that you don't miss what He wants you to learn.

All of life is a test. God watches to see how we respond to people, problems, success, conflicts, illness and disappointments so that He can mature us as His children. One of my favorite verses is Psalm 50:15, *"Call upon me in the day of trouble; I will deliver you, and you will honor me."* I have called on the Lord many times, and I love giving Him the glory and praise in the midst of my trials when He delivers me.

A Trial Causes Us to Trust

It's important to call on God first whenever we enter a crisis. He has promised us that if we turn our problems over to Him, He will take them and handle them. He gets glory when we trust Him and call on Him. As we grow closer to the Lord, we discover how many things God has done in us and for us. In other words, He is constantly changing us. God is taking away our old habits and attitudes and making us more like Christ. We will continue to grow and mature in our walk with God if we continue to trust Him.

A trial can teach us to trust that God has greater plans for us than we can imagine. He will take us to the next stage, and we will become more mature. Sometimes God uses us for the good of others so they can see what Christ is like, but everything is ultimately for His glory. God's purpose for us while we are on earth is to glorify Him. We can glorify Him by trusting Him to be who He says He is. It's not about performance; it's about trusting Him. Unless you fully trust Him, all your knowledge about the Bible and even the Scripture that you memorize is worthless unless it enables you to trust Him.

If you are going through a trial, maybe it's not about you. What if the Lord is training you for something down the road?

My dad died of cancer when I was 28 years old. He was 57 at the time. Most of my friends still have their parents, but several have passed away recently. Since I have been there and experienced that, I've been able to show compassion for others and comfort them when they've lost one of their parents. It's not something I wanted to experience at 28, but I believe there is a reason for everything and a purpose in pain. What I went through allows me to comfort others in a similar situation or in any need.

Second Corinthians 1:3–4 says, *"Praise be to the God and Father of our Lord Jesus Christ, the Father of compassion and the God of all comfort, who comforts us in all our troubles, so that we can comfort those in any trouble with the comfort we ourselves have received from God."* After I read this, I realized how many people I've been able to comfort because of my loss.

I think these verses are very clear. God comforts us during our trials, and then we are able to comfort our friends during their trials as God has comforted us. He gives the strength and comfort to get us through our trials, and then we are able to help others who might be in a similar situation.

Sandy taught me a prayer in October of 2002 that gave me confidence in being able to trust in Him:

Lord, everything that touches my life, every trial, crisis or dilemma, I want you to take them. I need you. I need your wisdom. I'm trusting you for this. Amen.

God comforts us in all our afflictions. He is the One who is willing and able to comfort us, and He desires to do it. However, sometimes we don't let Him. Unless we turn to Him and acknowledge that we need Him, we pass up an opportunity to receive His comfort.

He tells us that we need to come to Him during our trials and afflictions. He will comfort us right in the middle of the heaviest parts, when we feel like we don't know what to do. I remember wondering, "Why does the God of all comfort let His children have problems?" Have you ever wondered why He allows us to go through the trials and *then* comfort us? Why not let us detour around the problems?

If Christians had no problems, then everyone would want to be one. However, Christians clearly have problems, too. One of the reasons God allows Christians to have problems is for others to see how we handle them. Whenever we trust Him and give our problems to Him, they see that we depend on the Lord's help to deal with pain. As a result, they want to experience what we have in our lives, and they will be drawn to God through our example. When others are searching for answers, we get the opportunity to share the love of Christ with them. It's important to know that what we are recommending is truth, because we've lived it.

Let God run your life. He knows what is best for you. That doesn't mean you won't have any pain or suffering. However, remember that difficult times can help us get to know Him. God's will is good. When He takes us through problems, they may not seem good to us at the time, but if they are God's will then they have to be good. We should embrace His will and say, "Okay, Lord. If that's your will, then I'm okay with it," rather than grumble and say, "Okay, Lord. I'll submit." Be *willing* to choose God's will; that should be what you want.

Psalm 32:8 offers a comforting verse that reminds us to trust in God. God promises, *"I will instruct you and teach you in the way you should go; I will counsel you and watch over you."* As you read God's Word and come to know Him more intimately, He confirms that He is with you in big and little ways. These confirmations come with inner peace when you are making decisions or just living your life! That helps you to trust Him even more.

A Trial Is a Temporary Assignment

The good news is that all of life's trials are temporary—they won't last forever. However, it's important to see them as special assignments in your life.

Sandy once taught a class titled "Unshakable Faith." I want that kind of faith when trials or difficult times come my way. I want to be prepared to handle the assignment God gives me in the best way—not only for me, but mostly for those around me who are watching to see how I'm going to handle my trial.

Faith becomes reality during trials, not only to us but to those around us as well. As Christians, we always need to display our faith, but especially during hard times. We must live out our faith and let it be evident in the midst of our trial or "assignment." Jesus said in Matthew 6:33–34, *"But seek first his kingdom and his righteousness, and all these things will be given to you as well. Therefore do not worry about tomorrow, for tomorrow will worry about itself. Each day has enough trouble of its own."* We don't have to know a great deal of Scripture in order to have strong faith. Faith is simply the willingness to relate to and trust in the Lord.

Three C's of the Christian Life

I divorced in 1997, several years after my dad's death. I decided to stay in Dallas with my family and try to begin a new life as a single woman and develop my career as a photographer. My meetings with Sandy couldn't have come at a better time. She helped me understand what it meant to truly commit to the Lord and know Him intimately. Sandy described it as the "Three C's" of the Christian life.

Sandy taught me that the "Three Cs" of the Christian life are: concept, confidence and commitment. **First, we must have a clear concept of God.** We need a foundation for our faith. Our concept of God comes from Scripture, and it tells us who He is. This is why Sandy always encouraged me to know what God's Word said about the God I could trust. A healthy concept of God means knowing the truth about God. The better you know Scripture, the more wisdom and knowledge you will gain about God.

The more you know about God, the more you will be prepared to trust Him. You will also be prepared for questions from others or a crisis that might be around the corner. Knowing God gives you confidence in your heart, mind and soul and allows you to know the truth that He has written down for us to learn.

Second, concept forms the basis of confidence. Confidence means trust in God. When you have trust in God and believe in Him, your confidence should grow strong. If you know scriptures and believe they are true, that will build confidence in you that you've never experienced. God gives us confidence through knowing His Word. Confidence in God enables our commitment to God.

Remember the story of David and Goliath? David was an average man up against a giant. The only weapon he had was a slingshot, but his confidence was overflowing! He knew God was beside him and would protect him because he believed in God. He was confident that no matter what happened, God was in control. That strong faith and abundant confidence was remarkable for a young boy looking up at a huge giant engaged in war.

Until you can release a crisis, you haven't confirmed your confidence in the One you say you believe. This gives God an opportunity to prove to you that He is all He has claimed to be, and you really get to know Him in a practical way. The more you know Him and the closer you are to Him, the smaller everything else appears. In fact, the Bible says in 1 Corinthians 2:9, *"No eye has seen, no ear has heard, no mind has conceived what God has prepared for those who love him."*

Third, commitment means giving everything, including your problems, to God. You must commit to Him. Sandy helped me understand that committing confirms your confidence. Whenever you hear someone encourage you to "commit to God" it's another way of saying, "follow Him." Give Him your worries, your anxiety and your situations that seem like they have no solutions. First Peter 5:7 says, *"Cast all your anxiety on him because he cares for you."* Commit to Him and put Him first in your life.

Commitment means giving Him priority. When you ask Him to take over a problem or a situation in your life, don't try to take it back and fix it. God works in His own time, so don't rush Him. Just because He hasn't "fixed" your problem right away, don't try to take it back. Wait on Him. Psalm 46:10 says, *"Be still and know that I am God."*

Commit to Him, and be confident that He will be available to you because of your faith and trust in Him. Whenever you feel a sense of doubt or even outright panic about your circumstances, return to what you know to be true in Scripture. He loves us and will take care of us. Your knowledge from the Scriptures will allow you to have confidence and commit more and more.

So, be sure to have the right "Concept," which means knowing the "Truth about God" (Knowing the scriptures). Second, ask God to develop "Confidence," the ability to "Trust in God" (Believing in Him). As a result, you will practice "Commitment," which means "Entrust to God" (Giving everything to Him).

How the Class Began

I was by now a regular in Sandy's class, and it became like a habit I could not live without. Sandy related timeless truths from God's Word in a way that made me feel as though she was speaking right to me. Her stories and examples from Scripture fit my needs and situation so perfectly that it seemed as if God told her exactly what to say to me.

It wasn't just her teaching that was attractive. Sandy had a peace about her. The way she spoke conveyed authority and confidence that the Lord had given her. I wanted to sit at her feet and crawl into her lap at the same time. Most of all, I just wanted to hear more and learn what the Bible teaches us about everyday things.

This weekly Bible study started decades ago when Sandy moved to Dallas. She met her neighbor, Betty, and they became good friends. Not too long afterwards, Betty asked, "Would you consider teaching a Bible class for my daughter and some of her friends?" I'm sure Betty realized that Sandy had a heart for God and knew that she'd be a great person to lead the girls.

Sandy chose a wise response when she said, "Well, that would be fine, but I'd like to meet with their mothers so I can tell them what I'm going to teach on and answer any questions they might have. I want them to know that I'm not promoting any church but teaching them how to know Christ." Sandy continued, "I can teach them to trust God's will, how to pray and expect answers and how to have confidence in the Word of God." Sandy was particularly passionate about building a firm foundation of faith for young people so that someday when they were challenged or heard a different point of view, they would know *why* they believe what they believe.

Betty set up a coffee with all the mothers, and Sandy met them and explained to them what she intended to teach. When she was finished talking, she asked, "Are there any questions?" Silence. No one seemed to know what to say. Were they upset? Did they not want Sandy to teach their children?

The answer came with a smile when one lady raised her hand and boldly asked, "I have a question. Will you teach us?"

That was in 1963. The Bible study started in a friend's home and when there were so many women that they outgrew the home, they moved to Grace Bible Church. She has taught and discipled many women over the last 45 years. She has been a stable and strong source for several people, and she has given each one confidence in the Lord. He has taught us through Sandy and used her as His vessel to relate the promises of God's Word to us. Sandy told me, "If He sent me, He will enable me, and He gets the glory." I believe Sandy has given God lots of glory, and she continues to do so today.

God Teaches through Trials

As Christian believers, we need to share our experiences and life lessons with others. Your personal testimony can be much more effective to someone than a sermon at church. People can relate better if they hear your story and what you learned from it or how the Lord worked in your life. Not only can we learn from our trials and mistakes, but we can also learn from other people and their life lessons as well. Proverbs 25:12 says it plainly: *"A warning given by an experienced person to someone willing to listen is more valuable than…jewelry made of the finest gold."* (Good News Translation)

One of the things I began to learn in her class was to pay attention to what God is doing in our lives. Whether we are going through good or bad experiences, most of us learn more from our difficulties than from good times. Sandy has always said that it's the difficult times and trials that lead us to the Lord.

The most difficult experience I ever had was holding my dad's hand when he took his last breath. During his last three days, I was in constant prayer. If I hadn't been, I know I would not have made it through as well as I did. The Lord brought me a supernatural peace. Sandy taught me that whenever we are going through hardship above our ability, we qualify for God's all-surpassing power. He provides strength, encouragement and comfort at that time.

The Bible says in 2 Corinthians 4:7–9, *"But we have this treasure in jars of clay [frail and fallible human beings] to show that this all-surpassing power is from God and not from us. We are hard pressed on every side, but not crushed; perplexed, but not in despair; persecuted, but not abandoned; struck down, but not destroyed."* (parentheses added)

The Scripture here is very clear that God wants us to rely on Him in *all* our circumstances. In 2 Corinthians 1:8–9, Paul relates his hardships to us so we can learn from his experiences. He writes, *"We were under great pressure, far beyond our ability to endure, so that we despaired even of life. But this happened that we might not rely on ourselves but on God..."* When we are in a major calamity, we qualify for God's unexplained peace and comfort.

Perhaps you have watched a friend in a difficult circumstance who tried everything but God in order to get some relief. I've heard friends say, "Well, I tried this or that. Then I went to a therapist and tried that. I guess I'll pray about it." That's what God wants us to do in the first place! Put God first, not last.

"Everything happens for a reason" is my life's motto, and Romans 8:28 confirms this principle. It says, *"And we know that in all things God works for the good of those who love him..."* Whether we realize it or not, God is in control. He doesn't look down and say, "Oops, I didn't mean for that to happen to Sally." The Lord knows about everything—good and bad—even before we're born.

He *allows* problems to come into our lives so we will come to Him and trust Him. He knows He can handle these situations, and He also knows that we cannot. In fact, He designed us to be inadequate in ourselves and to be dependent on Christ. We need Him, and we must have a moment-by-moment dependence on Him. As believers, we have access by faith to Christ, who is always sufficient and available to us. We have to trust Him to be our sufficiency, and when we do, He will enable us to function beyond our human ability. He asks us to have faith in Him, and He promises to help us so that we are confident that we don't have to live our lives alone.

Sometimes when problems happen to us (or to our loved ones) our first reaction is to ask, "Why?" However, as time goes by, we begin to see, understand and experience what God is doing. God wants to transform us into the image of His Son, and we need to be willing and ready. After we choose eternal life as God's children, He gives us a wonderful opportunity to get to know

Him and have life in Him so that we will not succumb
to the pressures of being human (what the Bible calls
"the flesh").

The older we get, the more experience we accumu-
late. Let's hope that those experiences have drawn us
closer to the Lord and that we will develop a close relationship with Him through prayer. It's so important that
we trust in God. Turn your problems over to Him and
He will provide faith and confidence. But watch out…
just about the time you are ready to turn your problems over to God, Satan will often convince you that
you don't need any help. We all need help in life; no
one can succeed alone. Have you tried working through
problems without God? Let me ask you: How is that
working out for you?

Learn to renew your mind with information that God
has given to you through Scripture. In this way, you will
know truth when you hear it. Every day when you wake
up, be aware that you will probably encounter a situation you can learn from that day. In fact, each day has a
life lesson waiting, but we must have open eyes to see it,
open ears to hear it and open hearts to feel it. Before you
walk out the door each morning, pray something like:

*Lord, help me be aware of and attentive to what
is going on around me today. Allow me to have
open eyes, ears and heart so that I might be able
to learn more about You today through one of my
experiences.*

We know that some days run more smoothly than
others. However, learn to be thankful for the tough days

because that is when we are more likely to learn something important. The Lord is constantly shaping and molding us so He can use us more effectively. James 1:12 is also an encouraging verse because it reminds us that God blesses us through trials. *"Blessed is the man who perseveres under trial, because when he has stood the test, he will receive the crown of life that God has promised to those who love him."* We are blessed even when we are suffering.

The Knife Maker

I once heard a great story about knife-making and how God uses us and works through us during trials. A knife begins as an ugly piece of metal with no purpose. The knife maker puts it in an intense fire until it is white hot. Then he pulls it out and he is able to shape it by pounding it with a big mallet. When it begins to cool, he puts it back in the fire for a while longer, pulls it back out and begins pounding it again and molding it into the shape of a knife. When he is finished, the knife is a beautiful, useful tool that can now be helpful wherever it's needed.

God is like the knife maker, spiritually speaking. He puts us in the fire of trials and difficult times and then He pulls us out so He can shape and mold us. If we aren't quite ready yet (or we have not depended on Him or trusted Him), back in the fire we go. He repeats this process until He has shaped and molded us enough to be useful.

No matter what stage of life you are in, remember that God is in control. He is shaping and molding you so that He can use you for His purposes. While we are in the fire, we need to be in constant prayer and be aware of what the Lord is trying to teach us. Of course, we should always be in continuous prayer despite what we are going through, not just during trials. However, problems have a unique way of drawing us to our knees. He is all you will ever need in any situation you'll ever have. In our darkest hours we fully discover who He is.

The Correct Concept of the Christian Life

I know many devoted Christians who have gone through indescribably tough times. My friends Jean Ann and Reagan are an inspiring example. Years ago, their daughter took her life at the age of 19. To help them cope with their devastating loss, they completely leaned on the Lord. Seven years later, Jean Ann was diagnosed with Lou Gehrig's disease, and it has been extremely tough for them, especially Reagan. Jean Ann lost the use of her legs and arms, and now her breathing is becoming difficult without oxygen.

She and Reagan tell me that they know this is the Lord's will, and they are prepared to accept what will follow when her lungs shut down. Jean Ann's spirits are high, and she always has a smile on her face. She has even said she is looking forward to heaven and being in the presence of the Lord. She has given God the glory and is looking forward to her life in heaven for eternity.

Reagan is excited for her to be in the presence of the Lord, but his faith and dedication to God keep him from falling apart, realizing that he is about to lose his wife of 25 years. Jean Ann doesn't want to leave Reagan, but she knows they will be together again someday soon. Few people could stand up under such anguish, unless they were depending and leaning on the Lord to get them through their difficult circumstances.

The example that Jean Ann and Reagan give to believers is amazing. No matter how tough their circumstances are, they have kept their faith and depended on the Lord. They know He is in control, and they trust Him even during their crisis.

The Christian life doesn't mean we won't have problems, but we can have joy and peace in Him in the midst of them. When God has a way, no other way works! Sandy taught me what the Bible says about what to expect as a Christian.

1. Expect you will need Him all the way through.
2. Expect trials to prove who He is.
3. Expect Him to have a purpose in mind for you.
4. Expect benefits to be gained through trials.
5. Learn to lean on Him!

Paul assures us in 2 Corinthians 4:17–18 that no matter how insignificant or how drastic our problems are, the Lord is there for us, and we need to stay focused on Him at all times. Paul writes, *"For our light and momentary troubles are achieving for us an eternal glory that far outweighs them all. So we fix our eyes not on what is seen but on what is unseen. For what is seen is temporary, but what is unseen is eternal."*

A few verses later in 2 Corinthians 5:7 he reminds us, *"We live by faith, not by sight."* This is an especially meaningful verse because Jean Ann went into the loving arms of her Lord on August 8, 2005, less than a month after I started writing this book. Jean Ann and Reagan were a great illustration to others in how to cope during a crisis and depend on the Lord.

Living the Christian life like Jean Ann and Reagan inspires other people to want the life you have. They will want to know how you can cope in devastating situations. Sandy once said that it gives you an opportunity to say, *"I can do everything through him who gives me strength"* (Philippians 4:13). I put my trust and faith in the Lord, and He upholds me in times of trouble.

The closer you come to Christ, the more you know Him and the better your relationship becomes. This relationship gives you an advantage when the trials come (and they will come, so be prepared). The closer you are to the Lord, the easier your trials are to handle. James 1:5 says, *"If any of you lacks wisdom, he should ask God, who gives generously to all without finding fault, and it will be given to him."*

Learning More Lessons

After I had been in Sandy's Bible study class for several years, God had healed a lot of hurt in my life. I was learning so much about my faith and growing in my relationship with God with each passing year.

Sandy and I continued to meet, but our conversations began to revolve around a new turn in my social life—dating. God carried me through my divorce and Sandy had helped me process the experience to a point where I felt hopeful about my future again. Sandy does not approve of divorce, but there came a time in my marriage that it was inevitable. She still loved me even though I decided to end the marriage. I dreamed of meeting a godly man who loved the Lord as much or more as I did. If it wasn't too much to ask, I hoped that he enjoyed the outdoors like me and that he had an appreciation for the finer points of tennis and snow-skiing. However, the longer I was in the "dating scene" the more it seemed like finding a single godly man was more of an impossible dream than I'd anticipated.

*"But seek first his kingdom and his righteous-
ness, and all these things will be given to you as
well. Therefore do not worry about tomorrow,
for tomorrow will worry about itself. Each day
has enough trouble of its own."*
Matthew 6:33–34

*"If any of you lacks wisdom, he should ask God,
who gives generously to all without finding
fault, and it will be given to him."*
James 1:5

Chapter 4

God Has a Plan

Since the time that Sandy and I had started meeting together consistently, I felt that my spiritual maturity had developed immensely. However, just when you think you know it all, you can expect another reality check. (Of course, I know that you can never "know it all" when it comes to having knowledge of the Scriptures and following the Lord's will in your life.)

I had so much fun telling Sandy my "You're not going to believe this" stories about some of my dates. I remember one gentleman in particular. Over dinner, I casually asked him about his life and interests. I was trying to get a handle on what was important to him. After I asked him about his faith, he told me that he had been a Christian since he was eight years old.

"Oh really?" I said as I raised my glass and took a long sip of water. I was thinking to myself that this guy just might have potential after all. "Tell me about how that happened," I said and tried not to appear too eager. On all of my dates up to that point, I was always the one who steered the conversation to talk about church and faith. No guy ever took the initiative to bring it up.

"Well," he stammered, searching for words. I wondered why he suddenly seemed so nervous as though he'd never been asked about his faith before. He continued, "Well, I got baptized in front of the church." End of story. And, sadly, it was the end of our date as well.

For all his great qualities, he didn't realize that becoming a believer is not merely being baptized. He had never made a conscious decision by faith to receive Jesus into his life. I was very upfront about wanting a man who was as devoted to Christ as I was. I began to wonder if, at my age, all of the good ones were already gone.

After hearing some of my stories, Sandy reminded me, "All God asks of us as believers is to marry a believer." In other words, He doesn't say that Christians have to marry someone their age with blue eyes or brown hair or a good job. All He asks is that we marry a believer. If you don't marry a fellow believer, you will live in two realms—light and darkness—and they do not mix. There will be a whole area of your life that you won't share with your spouse.

Knowing this eliminated many potential dates right from the outset. In fact, I didn't really expect to meet that many men who met the basic requirement of being a committed Christian. And I sure didn't expect to meet someone who wanted to follow God as much as I did. That is, until I met Ben.

East Texas Charmer

In October 2003, I met a man named Ben. He was so darned handsome that I couldn't keep from staring at him. I was at a restaurant with about 10 other single people. My friend Kathy had invited me to join them, and someone she invited had invited Ben. It was one of those friend-of-a-friend situations and I knew nothing about him.

However, when Ben walked out onto the outdoor patio to join us, all I could think was, "Wow, who is that guy?" *(Eyebrow raise #1)*

We began to talk, and I immediately noticed his sweet disposition and East Texas charm. While we were chatting, I wondered, "How can I get his number? Or how can I give him mine?" It would have been awkward to exchange phone numbers with so many other single people around, so I decided to play it cool for the moment. He asked what I did for a living and I told him I was a photographer. He grinned and said he loved photography and that he had been a photographer in high school. *(Eyebrow raise #2)*

I know it was the Holy Spirit guiding me when all of a sudden, without having rehearsed it in my mind, I suddenly jumped to my feet and said, "Hey everybody, why don't you all come to my house Saturday night? (I hardly knew these people.) Everybody give me your phone numbers!"

Ben jumped to his feet, grabbed my hand and gave me his business card. I tried to be cool as I crumpled up the other numbers in my hand. I called him the next day and said, "Hi, I'm Amy, the photographer from last night." I ended up inviting him to a Halloween party. His two daughters would be busy trick-or-treating with their friends, so he said, "Great! What time?"

When we went to the party, we immediately met one of his close friends, who just happened to be married to a girl with whom I grew up. After the party, we went back to my place and I introduced Ben to the love of my life: Buster, my black and white Springer Spaniel. Ben seemed to love dogs and was so sweet with Buster, which won big points with me. As we sat and talked, he brought up the subject of his faith. "I became a Christian late in life," he told me. *(Eyebrow raise #3)*

My ears perked up and I asked, "Oh, so when did you become a Christian?"

"About 10 years ago," he began. "I'll never forget sitting in the front seat of my best friend's Suburban. I got down on my knees and asked Jesus to come into my heart." *(Eyebrow raise #4)*

My heart almost exploded out of my chest, but that wasn't all. I then asked him, "Have you ever read *The Purpose Driven Life?*" This was a life-changing book for me in my walk with Christ, so it was important to me to talk about it with him. To my delight he said, "Yes, I loved that book. I teach Sunday school at my church, and I pattern the lessons after it."

"That's great! Do you play tennis?" I asked, trying not to sound like a job interview.

"Yes. I love tennis." *(Eyebrow raise #5)*

While I was on a roll, I decided to go for it all: "What about skiing? Do you like to ski?"

"Yes, I grew up skiing. My parents had a house in Breckenridge when I was growing up." *(Eyebrow raise #6)*

I thought my heart was going to bounce onto the floor. I felt like saying, "Wait right here. I'm going to get a wedding dress and I'll be right back." Fortunately, I withheld that comment, but I knew in my heart that the Lord had brought Ben to me.

When Ben left that night, he pulled me close, looked into my eyes and said, "I wonder if this is a God thing."

"I sure hope so," I said, and out the door he went.

That was a big "ahh" moment for me. I couldn't believe it. I had found a cute, adorable guy who knew the Lord. He was the first guy I'd ever gone out with who brought up the subject of faith on his own—I didn't have to ask. He had read *The Purpose Driven Life* (which changed my life) and he liked tennis and skiing! But more than that, he liked Buster! I thought to myself, "It's too good to be true!" I was so excited because I believed that meeting Ben was indeed a "God thing" and that the Lord had brought us together.

Going to Maui

After a week of dating, Ben mentioned that he was going to Maui on an incentive trip with Microsoft. I mentioned that since I used to live there I could give him some tips on where to go. By the end of dinner, he had invited me to go with him!

I decided not to answer right away and said I would have to check my schedule. I got home and looked at the dates on my calendar. If I went to Maui, I would miss a couple of dates with some other guys and a party I was hosting.

I called my best friend, Cara, who said, "Amy, no one invites you to Maui. You clear your schedule and you go!"

She was right. I made plans to head to paradise with an adorable, polite Christian man. I called Ben and told him the news. He got my plane ticket, and I got my own room.

The seven days in Maui were so much fun. It was as if we squeezed four months of dating into one short week. There were no interruptions, no cell phones ringing and no plans except what we wanted to do. In Maui, I also learned that Ben liked scuba diving, sailing, watching the sunsets and riding the zip line— a few more things we had in common. *(Eyebrow raise # 7, 8 and 9)*

Telling Sandy about Ben

Before I went to Maui, Sandy and I met at Starbucks for coffee so that I could fill her in on my new guy. I told her everything about him and said that I had no desire to see anyone else. "Everything is falling into place for our relationship," I said. "Ben and I have so much in common." And it was true—for two people who didn't know each other before now, we shared a lot of common ground.

For example, I told her how he had been a student at Southern Methodist University with one of my closest longtime friends, Darin, (who gave him an immediate "thumbs up" when I asked him about Ben). Later we found out that Ben's father had escorted my mother to an ROTC banquet years before at SMU! I knew that what seemed like coincidences were really just God's orchestration of His plan for us, which ultimately led to our marriage.

However, when I told Sandy that I had decided to go to Maui with Ben for a week, I could tell she was a little concerned. I assured her that I had my own room and not to worry about anything. What she said next made a huge impact on my life. She looked me in the eye and said, "Honey, you can't lose the right guy by doing what the Lord would have you do." My lips pursed and I nodded my head. What a profound statement! I repeated it silently in my head and realized she was right.

If the Lord's will was for Ben and me to marry, I wanted to honor that and do what would be right in His eyes. Her comment reinforced my beliefs and allowed me to stay on the right track to honor the Lord in my life. In times of temptation when I was dating, I would often pray:

> *"Lord, please bind Satan from tempting me. Please keep him from putting these thoughts in my mind."*

Reading Scripture is very helpful on such occasions. Leaving your Bible open in your room, listening to Christian music—all these things deter Satan. He will move on to someone else who is weak and unprotected by God.

Sandy also talked to me about my idea of marriage. What was it? What was Ben's idea of marriage? That was extremely helpful to me, and it should be important to everyone who considers marriage. What is your idea of marriage? Does it match your boyfriend's? God must join you together. Marriage is difficult enough, but without God in your life and in your marriage, it will be one long journey. First Corinthians 7:28 tells us, *"...But those who marry will face many troubles in this life, and I want to spare you this."* The Lord warns us that marriage is tough, and we must depend on Him.

As a couple, you must have Him in the center of your life. You might float along for years and things may seem good on the surface. However, without Christ as the center of your marriage, be ready for the turbulence to come. If you are married to a non-believer, pray for him to have an open heart toward the Lord. Pray that the Lord will put someone in his life to lead him to Christ.

God has someone picked out for each of us. If you don't marry the one He intended you to marry, it leads to heartache. However, if you marry the one He wants you to marry, I can tell you that it leads to a blessing.

Marrying Ben

Ben and I married in October of 2004. Our wedding was exactly how I had envisioned it: just family and, of course, Sandy. We got married on the loggia of my parent's house. It overlooks a lake with three black swans and two white swans named "Samson and Delilah," which seemed to be performing as they swam back and forth. My favorite, precious niece, Adrienne, walked over to the ivy-covered bridge and threw dozens of rose petals into the water. (I consider Adrienne, "Little A," my own. She is Andy's daughter, and I love her as if she was my own. If I could pick a daughter, I would pick her!) It was an overcast day and a little cool.

During the ceremony, one of our favorite singers from church sang our favorite song, "I Could Not Ask for More." As she sang, I looked out over the backyard I'd grown up in just as the rain began to sprinkle lightly. Tears welled up in my eyes at that moment. It was so romantic: the song, the rain, the swans swimming through the rose petals. I truly could not ask for more.

I felt the Lord had given me a second chance, and here Ben and I were—together arm in arm—looking out over the most beautiful backyard about to say our vows. Bill Counts, our pastor, read this passage of Scripture from Ruth: *"Where you go I will go, and where you stay I will stay. Where you die I will die, and there I will be buried,"* Ruth 1:16–17. As he read it, I thought to myself, "What a great verse!" because that's exactly how I felt. I want to be with Ben wherever he goes, and then one day we will be buried side by side.

Toward the end of the ceremony, our pastor called Sandy to the front to pray for us and Ben's two adorable girls, Lauren and Maddie. We all huddled together in a circle. Sandy stretched out her arms and wrapped them as far as she could around our family. Her prayer was sweet and sincere, and as she prayed I began to cry once again.

Sandy's Prayer

Sandy's prayer was so special to me. She said:

"Precious Father, as Ben and Amy make these commitments to each other we join together and commit them to You. We pray that they might grow in their love for each other and grow together in their love for You. We lift up Ben and ask that he might have Your wisdom, Your insight and Your discernment...that he might make wise decisions, and that he demonstrate tender and understanding love in his leadership. And we pray he will guard this home by watching over it as a sacred trust, one in which You will be number one.

We pray now, Lord, for precious Amy and we ask that she might be an encourager for Ben. We ask also that she will bring into their home her loving, thoughtful, fun personality and her compassion. May she so permeate that home with the Spirit that it will be a favorite place to be and one they would choose to be when they could be anywhere else. And we pray that her life will continue to be that sweet aroma of the knowledge of Christ in every place.

We pray for Lauren and Maddie that they will know love in this home. We pray that it will become a place where they will come because there will be wise counsel, encouragement and understanding there. And we pray this will be a time when they will be bonded as a family. Father, we praise You because You put all this together. We pray that your protection would be upon Lauren and Maddie, and we pray that You would draw them into Your purposes.

We commit all of this family to you and we ask Your blessing upon Amy and Ben. We ask that You would bind them together in Your love forever, Lord, and that this marriage and this family will bring glory to Your name. In Jesus' name, Amen."

Knowing God's Will

When I married Ben, I knew that no matter what happened we would always be together. We will spend eternity in heaven together. After being married over three years, I'm happier now than I was when we were dating. I still have the "ahh" feeling as soon as he walks through the door. The Lord has truly blessed us and our marriage.

Given my experience in dating and now marriage, let me remind you to pray about this area of your life constantly—whether you are single or married. If you are single, pray for the Lord to make clear to you the person He wants for you. The second step is to pay attention to the signs. Be aware of what the Lord is doing around you. When the Holy Spirit does not guide you—and you make all the decisions—you take a huge risk. I realize that I am not a marriage counselor or therapist, but I speak from my experiences and share advice and wisdom from one who has seen and experienced more than I have—my teacher, Sandy.

I know in my heart, mind and soul that it was the Lord's will for me to marry Ben. There was no doubt in my mind, not even for a second. I truly believe the Lord gives us signs and we receive a "peaceful" feeling when we are dating or marrying the right person.

The more I found out about Ben when he and I were dating, the more assurance God gave me that he was the one for me. I remember when we were driving to Henderson to meet Ben's parents for the first time. As we approached the city, I saw a big, green interstate sign that read, "Landon Alford Loop"—which just happened to be Ben's father's name.

"Is that your dad, Ben?" I asked with a grin. I was thinking to myself, *Who is this guy? His dad has a loop named after him?*

Ben gave a shy smile and said that his dad had "some property" where the city wanted to put a loop. He had never said a word about this before, and that impressed me. I realized what a genuinely humble man Ben is and thanked God for his character. When we got to Henderson, he took me all around his family's farm and lake. For the first time, I was dating a guy who could take *me* somewhere fun. Before, I was always inviting guys *with me* to our farm. I was so excited that Ben and I shared this in common and that he could entertain me with the things I liked to do for a change! I considered it another sign from God.

Pay attention to the signs and the feelings. Step back and ask yourself, "Is God trying to tell me something?" You do not want to miss whatever the Lord wants to tell you. Consider why certain things have been brought to your mind. More than likely, it is God trying to tell you something.

Ask for God's Will in Your Decisions

Matthew 6:6 says, *"But when you pray, go into your room, close the door and pray to your Father, who is unseen. Then your Father, who sees what is done in secret, will reward you."* This verse teaches that we need personal time with our Father in heaven. Back in Jesus' day, religious leaders prayed out loud in front of people with many words so that everyone around would think they were holy. Instead of a spiritual exercise, it was as if they were putting on a show in order to get attention from the crowd. Prayer should not be about showing off or trying to appear to be holy. Such behavior indicates that your real audience is not God. Of course, there are times when praying out loud is appropriate, but at its heart, prayer is a private communication with God.

Matthew 7:7 is what some people call the A.S.K. verse: *"Ask and it will be given to you (A.); seek and you will find (S.); knock and the door will be opened to you (K.)."* Some people may say, "I've prayed and nothing happened." Sometimes people give a half-hearted effort toward God, and then they expect everything to go their way. (Especially after they "tell" God their plans.) Knowing God takes faith, trust, focus and follow-through, and Jesus assures us that we will be rewarded.

God's answer to our questions can be one of three different answers: No, Yes, or Wait. Like me, you have probably experienced each answer many times in your lives. Looking back, I feel as though there have been more "No" and "Wait" answers than "Yes" answers. Yet when I look back, I realize He was saving me from someone or something. Even today, if the answer to one of my prayers is "No" or "Wait," I know God has a reason. I might not understand why, but I can accept it because I know that He knows what is best for me.

Here are some great verses to think about when you are seeking God's will:

Jeremiah 33:3 says, *"Call on me and I will answer you and tell you great and unsearchable things you do not know."*

One of my favorite verses pertaining to "calling on the Lord" is Psalm 50:15: *"Call upon me in the day of trouble; I will deliver you and you will honor me."*

James 4:2 says, *"You do not have because you do not ask."*

Ask God and keep asking…if it's His will for you, He will answer you, "Yes." If not, His answer is then either "No" or "Wait." Remember Sandy says, "With God no appointment is necessary!" We don't always know what is best for us, but God does. He has the right to choose His timing, and at the right time He will give you even more than what you ask for. So, trust Him during the delays; there is a reason when He wants you to wait. Sometimes we see the reason; sometimes it takes years. In some cases, it may be that we won't know why until we get to heaven.

Sandy once asked me a great question to illustrate the principle that God knows best. She asked, "Would a mother hand her young daughter a sharp knife if the daughter didn't know what she was doing and could hurt herself?" Of course not! The same is true with our heavenly Father—like a loving parent, He knows what is best. When you pray, ask for the Lord's will to be done in your life because He is the only one who knows where your life is going. He alone knows the outcome of the last chapter in your life.

It makes sense to me to ask the Lord for His will to be done. That way I eliminate the "in-between things" that often only cause confusion, pain and/or heartache. Doesn't that make sense? He has the plan; you might as well jump in with both feet and trust that where He takes you is where you are supposed to be.

Hebrews 11:6 is another great verse about seeking God. It says, *"And without faith it is impossible to please God, because anyone who comes to him must believe he exists and that he rewards those who earnestly seek him."* Faith to me means believing that God is who He says He is. I also believe that He will do what He says He will do.

Sometimes I don't see results from prayer, but that doesn't mean my level of faith should drop. Sandy has often told me that when we are willing to entrust our concerns to Him, He gives us a supernatural peace. When you draw nearer to Him, He draws nearer to you.

As Sandy once said, "Do you think God has ever seen anything big? It's all small stuff to Him." Our problems might seem huge to us, but they're small potatoes to our powerful God. Sandy always tells her class, "We can't lose! Do you realize the life that's available to us? It's an investment to call on Him!"

Praying According to God's Will

One of Sandy's classes on prayer was titled, "Praying According to God's Will." John 14:13–14 says, *"And I will do whatever you ask in my name, so that the Son may bring glory to the Father. You may ask me for anything in my name, and I will do it."* Sandy says that first of all you have to ask.

Second, you must ask in His name. There are many ways to pray using Jesus' name. For example, you might choose to say, "in the name of Jesus our Lord and Savior, or "the ruler of the heavens and the earth," or "the Lord who designed the universe" or a simple, "Dear Lord." "In Jesus' name" is not a phrase to tack on as a closing to our prayer. It is acknowledging that our access to the throne is only because we have a relationship with Him. It is His name that prevails with the Father. Pray with a heart open to God's will. We should desire and prefer His will in our lives, so we must ask for it in prayer.

Renew Your Mind to Find God's Will

Romans 12:1–2 explains how we can know what His will is and how to pray about it: *"Therefore, I urge you, brothers, in view of God's mercy, to offer your bodies as living sacrifices, holy and pleasing to God—this is your spiritual act of worship. Do not conform any longer to the pattern of this world, but be transformed by the renewing of your mind. Then you will be able to test and approve what God's will is—his good, pleasing and perfect will."*

In this passage, offering our bodies as "living sacrifices" means that God wants us to offer ourselves to Him, put aside our own desires and follow Him. It means to put our energy and resources in Him so that He can use us and guide us as He pleases. As Christians, God calls us to transform our minds. If we plant that truth in our minds (and in our children's minds) it's easier to avoid the ways and customs of the world like being prideful, jealous, selfish, stubborn and arrogant.

It's only when the Holy Spirit renews our minds, redirects us and educates us that we are truly transformed. I can validate this truth in my own life. The closer I've come to the Lord and have learned to pray for His will in my life, the more I've seen a difference in what I want. I have a different outlook on life now. Things that were important to me years ago are irrelevant.

I'm much more compassionate toward others than I ever was in the past. I don't "freak out" if I lose something material. For instance, if I spill something on my shirt or a rug in my house, I try to get the stain out, but I don't panic over it. Before, I would overreact and maybe even cry over something material. Not anymore! If it gets ruined, lost or destroyed, I remember it's only a "thing." I ask myself, "What do I value?" Then I think about the greater question, "What does God value?" I want to value what God values. Growing closer to God through prayer, circumstances, trials and difficult times in my life has changed my overall thinking. There are so many more important things to cry over than a shirt that was ruined, a rug that was stained or whatever it may be that you "love" so much. Nothing matters more in this world than your relationship with Jesus Christ, living His will for your life and understanding His purpose.

That is why it is so important for you to know God's will. I learned about God's will through my relationship with Ben, but His will applies in every area of our lives. Sandy taught me even more in this area, and I want to share with you what I learned about praying to know and do God's will.

"I will instruct you and teach you in the way you should go; I will counsel you and watch over you."
Psalm 32:8

"You do not have because you do not ask."
James 4:2

J.E. & SANDY EDMONSON
Grace Bible Church 1969

LARRY & ANNETTE FLECK
ANDY, AMY

Sandy and I shared the same page in our church
directory (1969) years before we met

Dad and me at my graduation from Brooks Photography
Institute (1988)

Spending time in Aspen with family (pictured: Mom and
my brother, Andy)

Dad helped me build a darkroom inside my attic in my home in Dallas

Last picture at the Ozark farm with Dad and Andy two months before Dad died

Ben and me on our wedding day

Ben and me with daughters, Lauren and Maddie

My favorite niece, Adrienne, "Little A"

Ben and me with my mom at my step-father Harold's
birthday

Harold and me on my birthday in Santa Barbara

Buster, the love of my life (before Ben!)

Celebrating Sandy's birthday

Chapter 5

Knowing and Doing God's Will

I can see God at work in my life in the way that he developed my photography business from the time I graduated from Brooks to my career today as a successful professional photographer in Dallas. I remember shooting my first wedding when I was a student at Brooks—I was more nervous than the bride! I took one 35mm camera and shot more than 15 rolls of film, praying the entire time that they would turn out okay. (It never even occurred to me in those days to bring a back up camera!)

When I was ready to get even more serious about my career, God planted a well-known Dallas photographer in my path to take me under his wing. I will always be grateful to John Haynsworth for taking me on as his assistant and helping establish my career. We first met in 1992 when he came to my mom's house to take a portrait of my mom and me to be in a book of donors for an animal charity. (I love animals.)

While he was setting up, I was asking him about his camera and told him about my training at Brooks. I had nothing to lose, so I asked him if he had any room for an assistant. He thought for a minute and said, "I've never had a girl assistant before...but, sure, call me tomorrow."

We worked together day in and day out for the next month, sometimes holding a dozen shoots a day. I dropped everything I was doing and cancelled any shoots I had just so I could be with this legend in photography and learn all that I could. I was the one making the kids laugh for children's portraits, holding the light disk and loading up the car. I did all of the grunt work, and I did it for free because I was learning so much. After a while, some people were calling me personally to do their portraits. I asked John at lunch one day about it, and I'll never forget his response. "There are enough people in this town for the two of us," he said. And I knew he meant it.

After a while, I had gained a good reputation around town in certain social circles, which led to some unique photo opportunities. My first "celebrity" photo shoot was at a fundraiser for George Bush, Sr. at a local Dallas home. I was one of only two photographers, and we had to go through security three hours earlier. Watching all of the secret service guys mill around, I was thinking, "This is the coolest thing," as I waited for the President.

Finally, he came out on the back porch of the home, where I was standing on the front row. Only a thin ribbon separated him from the crowd. At the end of the speech, he decided to come out into the crowd and shake hands near me. At the same time, the crowd pushed forward, pushing me directly into the President's chest! Here I was, smashed up against the President, chest to chest. I was so embarrassed and said, "I'm sorry, Mr. President, but I can't move!" He just smiled and kept shaking hands around and above me. After what seemed like an eternity, I managed to wriggle one of my arms out to the side to hold a camera and get a shot of me and the President smashed together. For all the trouble, I have to say that I took some great shots that day!

Since that time, I've photographed people whose names you might recognize like President George Bush, Jr. and his wife Laura, as well as Oprah Winfrey, Benjamin Netanyahu, Senator Kay Bailey Hutchinson and Bill Cosby. As I look back, I realize God brought me to this place in my life and career. There is no way I could have predicted what I am doing now way back when I was just a student developing my first photograph in a dark room. If you are young like I was then, it's hard to know what God's plan for your life will be. It's so important to pray and be patient for God's will to unfold in your life. He will bless you beyond your wildest dreams if you will just trust Him.

Praying According to God's Will

From the lesson on "Praying According to God's Will," Sandy gave us the following outline. When God's will is unknown, we must start with what we know to be His will.

- It is God's will that I pray.
- It is God's will that I pray about everything (especially anything that could provoke anxiety).

- It is God's will that I know His will.
- It is God's will that I have His wisdom to pray rightly.
- It is God's will for the Holy Spirit to direct my prayers in accordance with His will.

But what if you are unsure about God's will for your life? What if you're scared you can't do it? God is the source of everything, and He will enable us to do whatever He has called us to do. God will always give us challenges that are above us and situations that we think we can't handle. He designed us to be dependent on Him, so allow Him to be who He is in you. Look to Him for everything—every need and every desire. He is in control and can handle anything. Pray for your desire to be His desire.

When you're seeking God's will, be sure you are not twisting His words to suit your own needs and desires. I've met people who try to modify God's Word to make it more reasonable to them. They want to pick and choose what they want to believe. That is not what God intended us to do. He wrote the Bible for us to have as a guide and to teach us about Him. You can't flip through His Word, pick out the verses that you like and disregard the ones you don't want to obey or acknowledge. Every verse in the Bible is there for a reason. Every verse comes from God. Who is to say that we can pick and choose what to believe in order to accommodate our wants, needs and desires? A good prayer to pray is:

"Dear Lord, I pray that Your desire for my life will be my desire."

Be Ready to Obey God's Will

When you pray, *"Lord, I want to know Your will,"* be ready! You must have an open heart and be willing to follow His will for you. You can't ask for God's will, then check it out to see if it's going to fit into your plans! God's way will always be superior.

Sometimes the task God gives us seems impossible, but the only thing preventing it from coming to pass is our disobedience. God can't accomplish what He wants in our lives if we are disobedient. When you are struggling to know God's will in your life, consider these prayers:

Prayer: "Whatever your will is, Lord, please show me. I want to do Your will in my life." You must trust in Him and have confidence that He knows best.

Prayer: "Lord, give me the desire to do Your will, and give me the strength to carry it out. Help me to stay focused on what it is You want me to do."

The Devil Distracts You from God's Will

There are so many distractions in the world these days, mostly caused by Satan. He loves to throw us off course and cause confusion about what we know to be true. Just remember, Satan is trying to cause you to stumble every chance he can. He is the one who puts doubts in your mind.

Have you ever gotten up on Sunday to go to church and thought to yourself that staying in bed sounds better?

Or doing yard work or household chores? It makes the devil so mad when you decide to go to church. That means you are making God the priority and squashing the devil's attempt to keep you from going. Any time you desire to come closer to the Lord, the devil will very subtly distract you. Television, phone calls, you name it—he'll come up with it. He loves to keep us from knowing the Lord's Word and His will for us.

To prepare for these predictable distractions, Ephesians 6:10–18 tells us to put on the armor of God:

"Finally, be strong in the Lord and his mighty power. Put on the full armor of God so that you can take your stand against the devil's schemes. For our struggle is not against flesh and blood, but against the rulers, against the authorities, against the powers of this dark world and against the spiritual forces of evil in the heavenly realms. Therefore put on the full armor of God, so that when the day of evil comes, you may be able to stand your ground, and after you have done everything, to stand. Stand firm then, with the belt of truth buckled around your waist, with the breastplate of righteousness in place, and with your feet fitted with the readiness that comes from the gospel of peace. In addition to all of this, take up the shield of faith, with which you can extinguish all the flaming arrows of the evil one. Take the helmet of salvation and the sword of the Spirit, which is the word of God. And pray in the Spirit on all occasions with all kinds of prayers and requests."

These verses tell us plainly that we must be aware of Satan's schemes and be prepared to be attacked by the devil at any time. If you know Scripture and are strong in your faith, the devil gets discouraged. Sometimes he will go on to someone who is not as strong, someone he thinks he can push his way. Prepare yourself by memorizing Scripture, reading the Bible and learning more about what God wants you to do and be while you are here on earth. This discipline will help you be more prepared for the next trial.

Years ago, as my pastor's daughter Cindy and I were talking one day, I told her about having satanic dreams. Whenever I woke up after such a dream in the middle of the night, I felt a level of fear I had never before experienced. The room felt thick with evil; it was pressing me down. All I knew to do was pray. The feeling of oppression went away eventually, but not soon enough. It really bothered me for several days. Cindy explained to me that only the Lord knows your thoughts. He can hear you and know what you are thinking. The devil, on the other hand, does not know what you are thinking. He can hear you only if you speak audibly. If you say, *"In the name of Jesus, Satan, get out of my mind,"* he has to obey! I've said that many times, and instantly the fear has disappeared. Try it. It works.

From time to time, if I am feeling uneasy about something or I feel Satan is attacking, I'll say, "In the name of Jesus, Satan, get out of my head (or home)," and it lifts the heaviness I'm feeling. If you've never done it, I know it may sound strange. However, I encourage you to try it. For example, if you feel tempted by something you know you shouldn't be doing or thinking about, yell it out! It works!

The devil loves to confuse us; he is the master of distraction. He tries to keep us ignorant of the Word of God. His job is to keep us from having a relationship or communication with the Lord so that we will not know and do His will.

God's Will Is Not Necessarily Easy

Sometimes it's hard to pray for "God's will" to be done in your life. Sometimes it's not something you want to do. However, if it's the Lord's will, He will enable you to do it. God asks us to be obedient to Him, that's all. If we are obedient, then He will enable us to do His will.

Many years ago, my step-dad and mom were going through a ridiculously hard trial, literally. They were being sued for something that had not yet come to pass and was out of their control. In my opinion, the judge allowed the trial to happen for entertainment value because it was so ludicrous. She just wanted to see what would happen! My parents spent two months of their lives in a courtroom defending their future and standing up for what is right and wrong. My step-father is a man of integrity, good morals and values. He was not going to let others possibly destroy his company and values because of greed and self-centeredness. Harold has been such a great role model for me. I've learned so much from him about treating people with respect (even when they do not always deserve it) and giving to others who are less fortunate.

His mother and father instilled good morals and values in him when he was growing up. Harold became a Christian at the age of 12 in Golden, Texas. The church had a congregation of 50 and still does today! Most people who live in this little town of 150 people are farmers and school teachers. Harold pays the pastor's salary and has also provided the funds to build Golden's post office and school buildings and to put air conditioning in the school gyms!

When I first began to pray about this situation, I said, "Lord let us win." About two or three weeks into the trial, I changed my prayer. I started praying:

"Lord, I ask that Your will be done in this trial. If Your will means losing everything, please prepare me for what lies ahead."

For the next six or seven weeks, I prayed for the Lord's will to be done, instead of asking that we would "win the trial." When the trial was finally over, the Lord had answered my prayer. It was not in the way that I wanted, but in His way, which proved to be the best way. If we had won the trial outright, the other side would have appealed, again wasting another year of our lives. The verdict was a hung jury: three jury members for us and three against us. The outcome was that the attorneys settled the case in 36 hours. Both sides were pleased, and we never had to worry about it again.

A hung jury was something I never even thought of happening! The Lord was in control and He did it His way. This lesson taught me that sometimes we don't even know what to pray for. That's why it is best to pray for God's will to be done.

Sometimes You Make Bad Decisions

God wants to help you make decisions and know His will for your life. However, we will still make bad choices from time to time. You just have to learn from them. I know my mom and dad taught my brother and me to try and make the right decisions. However, my mom probably thinks she failed in that department. Especially when I would come home with videos and photographs of me sky diving and bungee jumping. My friends and I frequently recall hearing Mom say throughout the years, "Honey, *what* were you *thinking?*" I heard it so many times while I was growing up—we still mimic her saying it to this day! I can't say I've ever made the "right decisions" all my life, but I certainly learned from the wrong ones.

On one of my visits home from college, I was so excited to show my parents my latest adventure. I sat them down in front of the television and explained, "I want to show you something I did that I've always wanted to do."

Mom just said, "Oh no…" and I started the video. The opening scene was my roommate Kelly and I standing in front of a B-52 Bomber with parachutes attached to our backs. We were waving and saying hello to our parents. Mom didn't understand at first, not until my step-father Harold said with excitement in his voice, "You went sky diving!"

Mom put her head down into her hands. That was my first clue that I had made a bad decision. The only saving grace is that I lived to tell about it, although my landing was pretty painful to watch. The instructor had pulled me to the side during the training class and asked, "Do you want to use an advanced parachute?"

I said, "What's the difference?"

He replied, "You fall a lot faster"

Without hesitating I said, "Sure I will use it!" That was my second bad decision.

Just to give you an idea of how much faster I fell, Kelly jumped before me, and I landed about 15 minutes *before* she did. When I was about 100 feet from the ground, I was still going close to 80mph with my instructor behind me in a tandem chute. When we landed, I tripped and hit the ground so hard that I had grass between each tooth! My lip and knees were bloody, but I jumped up and said, "Let's go again!" (Thankfully, by the time my parents saw the video, my lip and knees had healed!) It truly was the most exhilarating thing I'd ever done. The free fall was a feeling I can't describe, and the whole experience left me wanting more.

However, Mom didn't say a word when the video was over. The next day, Mom and I were riding in the car. (She always drives because I drive too fast darting in and out of cars, and it scares her.) She said, "Amy, I want you to make me a promise right now. Promise me you will never sky dive again."

I tried arguing, "But Mom I joined the parachute club..."

"Amy, right now!" she said. And she meant business.

I never went sky diving again. I know God has a purpose for me, because there have been hundreds of opportunities for Him to bring me home. I'm sure all of Mom's prayers have had a lot to do with me making it back in one piece from one adventure or another.

There are decisions that aren't actually life-threatening, but if we choose poorly, they can take us down the road of heartache and pain. When I married the first time, I was only 24 at the time. We had dated about 10 years off and on. I prayed and prayed about this decision before I got married. I asked the Lord to "give me a sign" as to whether I should marry him or not. As I look back, the Lord gave me so many signs. However, I chose to ignore them. I went right ahead and did what I wanted to do.

That bad decision ended up being eight years of heartache for both of us. I learned from that experience, however. You can pray all you want for a "sign from God," but if your eyes and heart are not open to receiving His will for you, you will miss those signs. Just like I did.

We must be receptive and willing to accept God's will for us or we will face the consequences. If you pick and chose which part of His will you want to do, you might find yourself in a difficult situation. One of my personal prayers every day goes something like this:

"Lord, please help me to be God-centered, not self-centered. I don't want to be me-me-me all the time. Help me to see Your will and allow me to accept it and follow it."

Act on the Signs God Gives Us

We must pay attention to the signs God gives us and act on them. If you are in God's will, trust me, it will help divert you around even more difficulties. My dad told me back in high school to date only Christian boys. But I remember responding with a half-hearted, "Yeah, right, Dad."

If you're a teenager reading this, believe it or not, your parents have experience in dating, among other important things. Parents try to guide their kids in order to save them from going down the wrong path. Why? Because they love and care for their children. Somehow I always thought I was smarter than my parents, even though I was just 18. If I'd followed my parents' advice from the start, I would have saved myself from many difficult situations.

On the other hand, God allows some things to happen for a reason so that we will learn from our mistakes. Several years after my divorce, another guy came into my life. We were engaged, and I truly believed God had chosen him for me. As the wedding date grew closer, however, several "red flags" appeared. This time I paid attention! I felt the Lord was giving me signs, which turned out to be more like huge roadblocks. I took the hints from God after praying for about four days on my knees and shedding buckets of tears. I realized I was about to do one of the hardest things in my life. I called off the wedding.

People had already given us several wedding parties—really nice wedding parties. The wedding dress was altered and hanging in my closet. The wedding itself was less than a month away, and a couple more parties were right around the corner. I was ashamed and I didn't want to see anyone. I felt so bad about a lot of things, but there was no doubt in my mind: I could not make the same mistake again. After all the pain and embarrassment had subsided, I knew I'd made the right decision (especially after Ben entered my life). Next to receiving Jesus into my life, marrying Ben was the best decision I ever made, ever!

Dealing with Doubt

Proverbs 22:6 says, *"Train a child in the way he should go, and when he is old he will not turn from it."* I believe that verse because it happened to me. I've strayed from God, but I always come back to Him. I know He is the source and the foundation for all my needs.

As children grow older, they often hear about other gods and religions. You may be experiencing that right now if you are a young adult, or you may be a parent whose child is straying. If children are confident in their beliefs and have knowledge of Him, they can stand firm in their beliefs when others challenge their faith.

Especially if you are young, you might sometimes doubt Christianity—and that is okay. We all go through periods of doubt. I did when I was in college at the University of Arkansas. I was even attending a Baptist church at the time and I was a strong believer.

One day, I went to see the pastor, H.D. McCarthy. He just happened to be a good friend of my dad's from their high school days. I sat down across from him in his office and began to ask questions for which I didn't have the answers. I remember asking him things like, "What existed before God? Was it just black and void?" He read a verse to me in Genesis that answered my question, but what he said next stuck with me. He leaned forward, his arms crossed on top of his desk, and said, "Amy, there *are* Christians who doubt. As a matter of fact, it's not uncommon once you become a Christian to doubt." He handed me an orange and white booklet titled, "Doubting Christians." I took it home to my dorm room and read it in one sitting. It explained why we doubt sometimes, and it helped with that confused feeling I had.

Even though we might believe and have strong faith, it's perfectly human to feel like God has left us alone sometimes. We want to yell out, "Helloooo God! It's me...where are You?" He is always there for us, of course, even when we can't sense His presence. He promises us in Scripture that once we believe in Him and trust Him, He will never leave us. I've experienced times over the years (and maybe you have, too) when I'm so "on fire" for the Lord that I can't get enough of Him in my life. During those times, I would be in several different Bible classes a week, soaking up truth like a sponge because I am hungry to learn about the Lord.

Then there are times when I feel as though I would rather play tennis instead of going to Bible class. When I'm "on fire" for God, I wouldn't dream of skipping Bible class. However, there are times when other things take priority. My Bible Study Fellowship (BSF) leader once told me, "Amy you can't be 'on fire' all the time.

You will have peaks and valleys." I'm so glad she said that because at the time I was in a valley. I was just as relieved to hear that a peak could be around the corner…and it was. I've experienced many "peaks and valleys" over the years, and I have to say that I prefer the peaks!

Sometimes we may even doubt what the Bible says is true. A friend once said to me, "How do you know what the Bible says is true? How do you know a bunch of crazy men didn't write it?" She obviously had not taken the time to read the Bible or cross-reference it with historical facts. During one of Sandy's lessons on the Holy Spirit, she explained that all Scripture was inspired by God through His Spirit. I remember she told me once, "When I found out that Scripture was truly God's Word—that it wasn't a dull dry book, but that it was life—I wanted to know it."

Scripture was inspired by God to the men who recorded it. In addition, the apostles witnessed firsthand so many miracles that Jesus performed. The Bible says that as many as 500 people saw Jesus alive again three days after He was crucified, dead and buried (1 Corinthians 15:6). When Mary Magdalene and Mary the mother of James went to the tomb with spices to anoint Jesus' body, the Bible says, *"…she turned around and saw Jesus standing there…"* (John 20:14). It says the disciples also saw Him in John 20:19–20, *"… when the disciples were together, with the doors locked for fear of the Jews, Jesus came and stood among them and said 'Peace be with you!' After he said this, he showed them His hands and side. The disciples were overjoyed when they saw the Lord."* Jesus showed them His nail-pierced hands and feet to prove that it was really Him!

Acts1:3 tells us that Jesus proved to many other people that He had come back from the dead, just as He promised. *"After His suffering, He showed Himself to these men and gave many convincing proofs that He was alive. He appeared to them over a period of forty days and spoke about the kingdom of God."* These passages make me realize that each story recorded in Scripture has a certain message and a purpose to convey to us. That's why it is "inspired." God chose each verse and story to be recorded and inspired writers to write those particular ones. In fact, there are several things Jesus did that God chose not to include in the Bible. John 21:25 says, *"Jesus did many other things as well. If every one of them were written down, I suppose that even the whole world would not have room for the books that would be written."*

Check out what 2 Peter 1:20–21 says: *"Above all, you must understand that no prophecy of scripture came about by the prophet's own interpretation. For prophecy never had its origin in the will of man, but men spoke from God as they were carried along by the Holy Spirit."* In other words, the apostles were the "vessels" (the ones who carried His Word). Today, we have people like Sandy, Billy Graham, Luis Palau and other gifted pastors to deliver God's Word.

Learning More about God

One thing that has helped me in my relationship with Christ is to learn more about the Holy Spirit. When Sandy told the class that she was going to teach us about the importance of the Spirit, I could hardly wait. Sandy's lesson title was, "The Spirit-filled Christian." We all filed in as usual and found a seat. However, there was nothing "usual" about what we were about to learn.

"Come to me, all you who are weary and burdened, and I will give you rest. Take my yoke upon you and learn from me, for I am gentle and humble in heart, and you will find rest for your souls. For my yoke is easy and my burden is light."
Matthew 11:28–30

"Do not merely listen to the word, and so deceive yourselves. Do what it says."
James 1:22

"...His divine power has already granted us everything pertaining to life and godliness...so that by them we might become partakers of His divine nature."
2 Peter 1:3–4 (New American Standard)

Chapter 6

Surrendering Control

Have you ever wondered, "Am I a Christian?" If you have sincerely trusted Christ for your salvation and acknowledged Him as Lord, you are a Christian. (If you are not a Christian or you are unsure, look in the back of this book for information on "How to Become a Christian.") At the same time that we receive Jesus Christ as Savior, we receive the Holy Spirit. At that moment we are indwelt, sealed and baptized in the Holy Spirit.

Here are some other scriptures for you to study about the Holy Spirit:

Romans 8:9 says, *"You, however, are controlled not by the sinful nature but by the Spirit, if the Spirit of God lives in you. And if anyone does not have the Spirit of Christ, he does not belong to Christ."*

First Corinthians 6:19–20 says, *"Do you not know that your body is a temple of the Holy Spirit who is in you, whom you have received from God? You are not your own, you were bought at a price. Therefore honor God with your body."*

Ephesians 4:4–6 says, *"There is one body and one Spirit just as you were called to one hope when you were called—one Lord, one faith, one baptism; one God and Father of all, who is over all and through all and in all."*

Galatians 3:26–28 says, *"You are all sons of God through faith in Christ Jesus, for all of you who were baptized into Christ have clothed yourselves with Christ. There is neither Jew nor Greek, slave nor free, male nor female, for you are all one in Christ Jesus."* Once you receive Christ, you receive the Holy Spirit. We are all united with Christ and with all other believers. Your race, ethnic background and whether you are a girl or boy does not matter.

Being Controlled by the Spirit

The Greek word for "baptized" used in Galatians 3:27 means to dip something or someone or place into (like water) (Thayer's Greek Lexicon). We all have the Holy Spirit, but that doesn't mean we *are filled* with the Spirit. We need to give control of ourselves to Him. When you give up control of your life, God takes over and proceeds with His plan for you. Being filled with the Spirit means He takes possession of you (Thayer's Greek Lexicon). Baptism in the Spirit brings us into a relationship with Him. Filling brings us under His control. We are commanded to be filled with the Spirit. Be willing to submit, because whatever He has planned for you is far better than what we have planned for ourselves. I often pray:

"Lord, I want to embrace Your will for me. Lord, You choose for me, in all the decisions I need to make."

You make an eternal investment when you submit and give your life to God. We can't comprehend what is waiting for us in heaven. It will be above anything we can imagine. But for now, we have to learn to live here on earth in a way that honors Him. That's why we must be controlled by the Spirit.

Because we are Christians, God provides guidance for us that the world doesn't have. This guidance comes from the Holy Spirit within us who will prepare us if we are open and teachable. John 16:13 states, *"But when he, the Spirit of truth, comes, he will guide you into all truth. He will not speak on his own; he will speak only what he hears, and he will tell you what is yet to come."* The Holy Spirit will guide us if we are available to him.

Romans 8:32 says, *"He who did not spare his own Son, but gave him up for us all—how will he not also, along with him, graciously give us all things?"* We have all things in Him if we will just depend on Him. If you desire to let the Holy Spirit fill you, you need to reaffirm your position of surrender to His control each morning. Make it a consistent way of life. When you pray in the morning, tell God you are available to Him.

We also need to follow the examples God gave us in the Bible of what it means to submit to His control in our lives. Each story and verse has a reason (otherwise it would be not be in the Bible). Of course, Jesus is our ultimate example of submitting to God. Acts 10:38

speaks about *"how God anointed Jesus of Nazareth with the Holy Spirit and power, and how he went around doing good and healing all who were under the power of the devil, because God was with him."* We must submit to the Holy Spirit as Christ submitted to His Father. We must depend on God's power and acknowledge that we need His control.

Sandy taught me that we can be controlled by joy, peace and love or by jealousy, anger, bitterness and envy (things that are of the flesh and are not controlled by the Holy Spirit). She put it this way, "The Holy Spirit is a divine interior decorator like you can't imagine!" We got a giggle out of that, but she is so right! The Holy Spirit is always available to you, but you must let Him have control of your life. If you do, then He becomes your enabling power. Sandy is right—you can be controlled by something other than the Spirit, like anger. I've seen it firsthand.

When I was single, I once dated a guy who was handsome, smart and seemed to have it all together. The longer we dated, the more I learned about him and his family. Tragically, his mother had been murdered by her boyfriend. Needless to say, "Mark" had a very difficult time with that. By the time I came along, it had been a couple of years since the murder. Even so, during that time "Mark" continued indirectly to torture the man who killed his mom. I remember telling him, "The anger and bitterness you have inside will eat you alive. God will take care of [the boyfriend]. You need to ask God to give you peace about this, or you'll end up with an illness from all the anger that's built up inside you." I truly believe that intense anger and bitterness can eat you from the inside out.

It's unfortunate, but it can happen to you quite easily, unless you stay focused on the Lord. Romans 12:17–19 says, *"Do not repay anyone evil for evil. Be careful to do what is right in the eyes of everybody. If it is possible, as far as it depends on you, live at peace with everyone. Do not take revenge, my friends, but leave room for God's wrath, for it is written; 'It is mine to avenge; I will repay, say the Lord.'"* The King James Version of verse 17 says it a little differently, *"Recompense to no man evil for evil. Provide things honest in the sight of all men."*

I claimed that verse several years ago when someone did a huge injustice to my mom and Harold. From that experience, I can see how anger and bitterness can fester very quickly. Lucky for me, I was involved in Bible Study Fellowship (BSF) at the time and had a great teacher who showed me that verse. It settled me down pretty fast. (Another good reason to be involved in a Bible class of some sort!)

The Holy Spirit was there for me during that situation, and He gave me a change of heart. We all come across challenges throughout our lives. If you don't have the Holy Spirit guiding you inside, you can go down the wrong path so easily. Not only that, your whole life can get away from you. The Holy Spirit wants to be in charge of your life, and what a relief! Let Him have it!

The Holy Spirit Enables You

When Sandy began teaching us about the Holy Spirit you could feel her excitement throughout the room. One day, I was a few minutes early to class, so I poured myself some water and planted myself front and center. (I got there early so I could save seats for my friends.) As I sat quietly waiting, I asked the Lord to open my heart and ears to whatever He wanted me to hear that day in class. Just as I finished, I opened my eyes and saw Sandy coming from the room next door that was filled with sofas, games and chairs. I asked her, "What are you doing in there?"

"Oh, Honey," she said, "I always pray before class. I ask the Lord to speak through me to each one here." Then she began the class the way she always does by saying, "Good morning, girls!" We answered back, "Good morning, Sandy." She told me she prays before each class, and asks the Holy Spirit to speak through her to us. She asks that our hearts will be open and receptive to what the Lord is saying to us through her. That could be the very reason why her delivery is so good. Her lessons speak to each one of us in a different way, even though we all hear the same thing. I've never left Sandy's class feeling empty or confused. Sometimes it's a struggle to get to class, but I always walk away with something valuable and worthwhile.

It seems as though Satan can give you all kinds of excuses not to go to Bible class or church. That's why I want to share with you what I've learned about avoiding distractions. Anytime you are reading the Bible or listening to a sermon or Bible teacher, always ask the Lord to help you focus. You may want to pray:

"Please clear my mind and allow me to focus on what it is You are trying to say to me through these words or through this sermon. Let me see

*clearly Your message and help me apply it to my
life."*

I always like to pray a prayer like that because it
helps me get ready to listen and clear all the thoughts
bouncing around in my head.

So many people overlook the power of the Holy
Spirit, and most Christians don't have any idea what is
available to them through Him. If the Lord gives you
an opportunity to do something, He will enable you.
He is responsible to enable you to do things He asks
you. What a relief to know that you are not alone! He is
going to work it out through you! By being available to
the Holy Spirit, He will prepare you for any encounter.

This reminds me of the story of Moses. When God
asked him to lead His people out of Egypt he said, "No
Lord! I can't lead these people. I'm not a leader, so
you've got the wrong guy." However, it's not what *we*
think we can do; it's being open and available to the
Lord and letting Him do it through us. Sandy even said,
"I would have never thought that I would be teaching a
Bible class. I'm not a teacher!" Even so, the Holy Spirit
teaches us through Sandy every Thursday! Second
Samuel 23:2 tells us the Holy Spirit uses us to speak to
others. *"The Spirit of the Lord spoke through me; his
word was on my tongue."* Sandy is a perfect example
of that verse. (If you had the chance to hear her speak,
you'd agree.) The Holy Spirit puts the words on our
tongues.

One of my favorite stories in the Bible is when
Jesus has ascended into heaven and the Holy Spirit
comes upon the disciples. At that moment, all of them

began speaking different languages—languages they had never spoken before that day. Thousands of people were "utterly amazed," the Bible tells us. Peter preached God's Word and the Bible says, *"Those who accepted his message were baptized, and about three thousand were added to their number that day,"* Acts 2:41. This is a picture of the Holy Spirit's power. He spoke through the disciples and enabled them to speak in the languages of all the people there. By doing so, God orchestrated what was certainly one of the biggest baptisms in their day and most likely in ours, too!

Just imagine sitting at dinner with your friends that night and saying, "We led three thousand people to Christ today!" It's exciting to lead one person to Christ, but I can't imagine three thousand! That just goes to show that anything is possible when you have the Holy Spirit living in you.

The Holy Spirit Transforms Our Character

When the Holy Spirit takes control of your life, your character (your identity) is different. Imagine you had a bucket full of clean water. If you add drops of dye to it and dip a piece of white cloth into the bucket, the cloth will change colors. It's still the same cloth, but its character has changed. That's how it is when the Holy Spirit works in us. When we believe in Jesus and receive Him into our lives, He sends the Holy Spirit to indwell in us. His presence changes and transforms us to be more like Christ.

Some people have said to me, "I will ask Jesus into my life when I get it straightened out." Jesus is the one who will do that! He didn't say, "Try harder and straighten up! Get all your problems fixed, then I'll come into your life." No, He knows we cannot live life on our own power. The Holy Spirit makes us holy and transforms us. There is no way we can do it on our own. The Christian life is not our "living our best" or our "doing our best." God has given us the Holy Spirit as the indwelling presence and power enabling the life that we cannot live to be lived in and through us. Galatians 2:20 says, *"I have been crucified with Christ and I no longer live, but Christ lives in me. The life I live in the body, I live by faith in the Son of God, who loved me and gave himself for me."*

I've also heard some people say, "Jesus could never love me. I have done the most horrible, unacceptable, vile things in my life and to my body. There is no way Jesus would forgive me for what I have done." Unfortunately, a lot of people think that way, but it's not true. That is why it is so important to read and learn Scripture so you can know the truth. It tells us in the Bible that Christ was the ultimate sacrifice for *all* our sins. It doesn't make exceptions as if forgiveness is available "just for that sin" or "just for him or her."

The Bible says God forgives *all* your sins when you accept Christ and believe He died on the cross for your sins. Christ is our mediator. We have a direct line to God; we don't need a person to mediate for us. If we ask Him to forgive us, He will. One of my favorite stories from Sandy is when her husband had just passed away. She walked into the waiting room in the hospital and sat down. One of the nurses walked up to her and said, "Ma'am, can I get you a priest?" Sandy said, "No thanks, I have a direct line." We all have direct lines to God.

I picture Christ as the ultimate Dad, sitting in heaven with His arms open wide and a smile on His face. He loves us no matter what we do. I know I have disappointed Him many times, but I also know that no matter what I do, He loves me and is always there for me even when I "flub-up."

Nobody is perfect, and there are many examples in the Bible of people who sinned. There are those who continued to do the wrong things like David, who was a murderer and adulterer. Peter continued to make the wrong choices and even denied Jesus. Paul went against Him! I am not saying they didn't suffer the consequences of their wrongdoing, but God allowed them to learn valuable lessons from the bad decisions that they made.

The Holy Spirit Is Powerful

When I lived in Maui, I found a Baptist church that I enjoyed, especially since the pastor was from Austin, Texas! I went to Lahina Baptist Church every Sunday and sat by myself. I also became friends with the pastor, Rudy, and his wife, Sarah.

It was an open-air church with latticework walls and held about 100 people. It was never full, but Rudy had a heart for God and it showed. There was no air-conditioning in the church, so most people wore shorts and sundresses. As time went on, I met two "howlie" girls named Amy and Michelle. ("Howlie" is a nickname the Hawaiian locals call the white people.) After church one day, I asked in my best Texas accent, "Where ya'll from?"

To my surprise, they answered, "Tyler, Texas." What are the chances? We became fast friends. (Us Texans like to stick together!) A few months went by and I began meeting more and more people in the church, including one girl named Betsy who was very involved as a leader in the youth group. We became friends and she invited me to be a camp counselor for a week at summer camp. Wow! That sounded good to me, and I began thinking about all kinds of fun tricks I could play on the campers. (I was 24 years old, but I was living like a 15-year-old!) Betsy told me there would be another church group joining us—25 kids from Arlington, Texas. Yea, more Texans!

Before camp, they prepped the counselors about the kids that would be going with us. The ones from Maui were pretty much non-believers. The ancient beliefs of the Hawaiians certainly didn't coincide with what the Bible teaches. However, we were told that the kids from Texas were all believers. It was definitely an odd mixture, like oil and water. Our mission? It was to have fun, but to lead the "Mauian's" to Christ and teach them about Christianity.

The Texans had nothing in common with the islanders…that is, until the night of the shaving cream and water balloon attack! That seemed to break the ice a bit. Night after night, either Rudy or the other pastor from Texas would talk to the kids about Jesus after dinner. Nothing ever seemed to get through to the islanders, but then the Holy Spirit showed up one night.

Rudy had the Bible in one hand, and he used his other hand to keep his place. His voice grew louder and louder as he confidently preached God's Word. I was sitting in the back of the room with Betsy and another friend named Kim on top of a big carpeted block of wood. From that vantage point, I looked around the room and noticed several kids crying. All of a sudden, I felt an energy sweep through the room. I knew exactly what it was.

The Holy Spirit was in the room and I felt Him all around me. The next thing I knew, the kids who had been crying were running back to us as fast as they could and saying, "We want to know Jesus." Tears began to stream down my face as I realized what was happening. This was an incredible moment! The Holy Spirit was right there in the room with us. What an awesome time to witness that He can move anyone's hearts—even those who seem so defiant.

I turned to Betsy and Kim who also had tears running down their faces as well. We looked into each other's eyes and I said, "Do you feel it, too?" They both nodded and we smiled as the children crowded around us. All the while, Rudy kept on preaching! I've looked in the dictionary for a word to describe what we experienced that evening. Nothing even comes close to describing what we felt that night. All I know is that there is no mistaking a room filled with the Spirit. Betsy and Kim confirmed what we all experienced.

After the meeting was over, I ran to the nearest pay phone to call two different people (no cell phones in those days!). I wanted to share what I had just experienced! Neither of the people I called was very excited.

I tried to explain it, but there were no words. I hung up feeling fairly deflated after their non-response to my enthusiastic news. Later that night, I realized something. Nobody can understand the power and the feelings of the Holy Spirit when He is in the room with you. (Not to mention the fact that it sounds pretty crazy.) Unless you are a true believer or have experienced it yourself, it is difficult to understand.

I never told anyone that story until a couple of years ago. The reason I'm sharing it now is because the Holy Spirit is real, and He is with you all the time. I know that because I have experienced Him firsthand. You don't always feel Him or realize He is there, but He is. Over the years, I have felt the Holy Spirit several times, but nothing like the night Rudy preached to the "islanders."

Change Takes Time

Some people mistakenly think that once they become believers, they will change overnight. We need to cooperate with the Holy Spirit in order for a change to take place, and that takes time. The Bible describes being changed over time as *"being transformed into his likeness with ever-increasing glory..."* (2 Corinthians 3:18). He will change you as you are willing. When we live our lives under His control, we have access to His peace. I've walked with the Lord long enough to know it's real and genuine. I've experienced it and I've lived it.

The Holy Spirit is what Sandy calls, "The Christian's Dynamic for Changed Lives." She says that we must desire to know the truth. The Holy Spirit helps us understand what God is trying to teach us. God doesn't let us have "Spiritual Strut." You'll never reach a point in your life when you are totally "Holy." There is always a need for more learning and more transformation. In addition to understanding the role of the Holy Spirit in my life, one of the most important lessons I've learned is how to pray to God.

"You, however, are controlled not by the sinful nature but by the Spirit, if the Spirit of God lives in you. And if anyone does not have the Spirit of Christ, he does not belong to Christ."
Romans 8:9

"Do you not know that your body is a temple of the Holy Spirit who is in you, whom you have received from God? You are not your own, you were bought at a price. Therefore honor God with your body."
1 Corinthians 6:19–20

Chapter 7

Praying with Power

Why is prayer important? It's the way we communicate with God and improve our relationship with Him. Romans 8:31–32 tells us, *"If God is for us, who can be against us? He who did not spare his own Son, but gave him up for us all—how will he not also, along with him, graciously give us all things?"* This verse tells us that when we have Christ, we have *everything.*

First Peter 3:12 says, *"For the eyes of the Lord are on the righteous and his ears are attentive to their prayer..."* The Lord does listen to our prayers. Not only that—He hears them *and* answers them! Remember—whenever there is a delay in the answer, there is a reason. Either the Lord is going to teach you something, or He has a better plan for you. Romans 8:25 says: *"But if we hope for what we do not yet have, we wait for it patiently."* Sometimes God answers your prayers in a different way from what you requested. Then you will know that the outcome fits God's plan; it is His will for your life.

When you ask the Lord something, be aware of what is going on around you so that you don't miss what He is trying to teach you. Ask Him to open your eyes so you can see clearly. Once you have received Jesus into your life, He lives in you and through you; this is where your relationship starts. He can transform your life, beginning with prayer.

Claiming Our Unclaimed Privilege

One day I walked into Bible study class and Sandy was already at the podium. I sat down quickly and grabbed a pen to learn about what she called, "claiming our unclaimed privilege." She explained to us, "The Lord loves it when we come to Him. He is accessible to us all day long. He cares about every little detail or care that we have. He wants us to come to Him with our needs, sharing our hurts when the pressure is too much and our joy when we are happy. He wants to be involved in every area of our lives."

Scripture describes our relationship with God as a father/son or father/daughter relationship. He desires us to have an intimate fellowship with Him. When my dad was ill with his cancer, I was drawn to the Lord by a constant flow of prayer. I have since learned that God communicates with us even though we don't hear an audible voice. I've had many experiences when God has communicated to me without speaking.

People often tell me, "I don't know how to pray." That's okay; it's you and God! Romans 8:26 tells us, *"...the Spirit helps us in our weakness. We do not know what we ought to pray for, but the Spirit himself inter-*

cedes for us with groans that words cannot express." In other words, the Holy Spirit will direct our prayers; He helps us and directs us according to the will of God.

About a month after Sandy spoke on, "Prayer According to God's Will," she taught us a lesson on, "Faith and Effectiveness of Prayer." She told us all kinds of good stuff! For example, she told us, "Prayer is God's alternative to anxiety." From time to time, Sandy starts the class by saying, "When God has a way..." and then the entire class finishes with, "...No other way works!" She has another memorable saying: "Everything is to be included in prayer, so that everything can be relinquished into His care." God allows us to have needs so that we will come to Him and He can fulfill them.

The Importance of Prayer

Prayer is communion with your Creator. It is by far one of the most important things you can do. Pray that your will for your life will be only the Lord's will. Don't forget to "be still" and listen to what God might be saying to you. Psalm 27:14 says, *"Wait for the Lord; be strong and take heart and wait for the Lord."*

I saw the power of prayer up close during a life-changing trip to Israel with my church. Being in Israel brought the Scriptures to life for me. While I was there, I had a peace in my soul that "surpasses all under-standing," that Paul wrote about in Philippians 4:7. It is hard to explain, but the other people who were there on the trip could feel it, too. Since I returned, reading the Bible has so much more impact on me. I can see in my mind where Jesus was crucified, buried and rose again. We saw the Temple Mount and the Mount of Olives, where Jesus will return at the Second Coming (Zechariah 14:4). The Wailing Wall in Jerusalem, where the Jews come to pray, was my favorite place to see.

I'll never forget walking through the old city, coming around the corner and seeing the wall before me. Everything began to move in slow motion at that moment. The sounds around me (including my own footsteps) were blurred and tears began to stream down my face. It was beautiful. The old walls from thousands of years ago still remain intact today. I thought to myself, "These are the same walls that Jesus walked by every time he was in the city." Nearby was the Dome of the Rock on the Temple Mount. I had seen the gold dome in photographs and on television, but seeing it in person was amazing. I felt as though my whole life was right before me.

I walked past many men with machine guns to get near the Wall and the Temple Mount. I never knew that the Wall is divided by a chain link fence separating the men from the women. I saw mothers tightly gripping the fence as they watched their little boys and husbands conduct their traditional Jewish ceremonies on the men's side of the barricade.

As I looked around, I saw hundreds of people praying out loud. Some had their hands in the air, while some were holding their faces with their hands. Most of the women had black scarves covering their heads with grey or dark colored skirts. A lot of the Jewish men wore black, round-rimmed hats with their locks of hair curled down in front of their ears. All the men were in black suits. Many women were praying, bending at the waist and swaying back and forth. They were making "wailing" noises, as if they were crying out to the Lord. Now I know why they call it the "Wailing Wall."

There were thousands of cracks in the wall. Each crack was stuffed with pieces of paper that had prayers written on them. The people, including myself, wrote their prayers on a small piece of paper, folded it up as small as possible and placed it on top of several other prayers inside the cracks. Afterwards, I put both hands on the wall and said a long prayer. With tears streaming down my face, I prayed in a whisper, "Lord, thank you for the opportunity to be here and feel Your presence over me." The presence of the Holy Spirit was so thick all around me. That was another "ah-ha" moment for me, one I'll never forget. Prayer is a wonderful privilege — we just need to use it.

Prayer Involves Praising and Thanking God

If you run out of things to pray about (not likely), be sure to thank Him for all your blessings. Remember the things you often take for granted and have never thanked God for, such as our cars, homes, beds, clothes and even shoes! Thank Him for the freedom to pray, learn His Word and worship openly on Sundays. Thank Him for your children if you are a parent. Thank Him for pets that keep us company, for food, water — the simplest things — and even for our minds. Remember to thank the Lord for everything you have. Praise and thanksgiving are just as important as our prayers!

One of my biggest life lessons came to my attention shortly after I married Ben and his two daughters became part of my family. Nothing like jumping into a family of teenagers! Many times, my husband and I have called our parents to tell them how much we love them and appreciate them. Many times when I'm at dinner with Mom and Harold, I thank them with tears rolling down my checks for loving me, caring for me and making me go on all those family trips when I was younger!

I never realized how important it is to tell your parents, "Thank you" until I had daughters of my own. I look back at all the times I acted like a brat and thought I knew everything. I remember my freshman year in high school, Mom and Harold announced they were taking my brother and me, along with my stepsister Lisa, to Rome, Florence and Paris for our summer vacation.

Mom had worked so hard on planning the trip and was so excited to take us to such fabulous places. She spent hours booking the flights, hotels and tours, getting all the right things together that she thought we would all enjoy. How did I thank her? I kicked and screamed, "I don't want to go to Europe and look at a bunch of old churches!"

Thank goodness she made me go. It was the most incredible trip I'd ever had! I learned more about history the first day we toured Rome than I had ever learned in school. I could hardly sleep at night thinking of what all I would see the next day. Not only did I learn so much, but it will always be a wonderful memory in my mind. Family vacations are always great memories and so much fun to talk about as we get older.

What I've learned over the years about appreciating my parents would not have been possible had I not had a family of my own. Luckily it's not too late to thank them and let them know how much I appreciate all they have done for me (and all they still do for me). It's so important to tell your parents, grandparents or whoever raised you, "Thank you."

Before my dad passed away, I was able to thank him for all he did for me—all the sacrifices, the love and the caring. (And for teaching me how to play sports!) I thought at the time that I had thanked him for everything possible; I was wrong.

It wasn't until recently that I realized how much it had hurt him all those times I blew off my dad for my friends. Because of my self-centeredness, there were many times I chose to be with friends instead of Dad. I would have dinner or lunch plans with him, and I would cancel at the last minute to be with friends. He never said a word, and he was always glad to see me when we would finally get together. Now he's gone, and I can't get that time back with my father. He loved me so much and wanted to spend time with me, but I was so focused on me and what made me happy that I missed hours of quality time with my dad.

Were it not for Ben and his girls, I would have never realized this. However, since I'm aware of it now, I spend as much time with Mom and Harold as I can. (Not to mention they are fun and we have a lot in common!) The point is to try to be appreciative for the things people do for you, especially your parents. Always take time to say or write, "Thank you, I appreciate what you do for me." In the same way, we need to thank the Lord for all He does for us! Don't let any blessings pass you by without praising and thanking the Lord.

Prayer Involves Praying for Others

Intercession simply means praying for others. This type of prayer can make an enormous difference in your relationships. For example, it can make a difference between you and your husband or you and your children. You can be the link that brings their needs to God. If God burdens you about something that needs prayer, then respond with faith. Let God take care of it.

Sandy once told us a story from World War I about a general in command of many forces in Egypt. He received orders to take over Jerusalem; however, the general was a Christian and did not want to bomb the Holy City. He knew that if he took his troops there, nothing would be left. He and his officers began to pray about the problem. Just before the attack was supposed to take place the next morning, a man walked out of the Holy City gates waving a white flag. The soldiers prayed again, praising the Lord for answering their prayers.

I think it is crucial for all of us to pray for our President, his cabinet, our government leaders, our generals and especially our soldiers. Every day! They are making decisions all day long that will affect our country now and forever. They need and appreciate any prayers we can give them.

A good time to pray or memorize Scripture is in the car. Put some verses on an index card and keep them on your visor or cup holder. Most of us have dead time in the car while waiting in carpool lines and at stoplights, car washes and drive-through bank lines. Prayer time in the car can be especially effective if you have young kids. Get them to read a Scripture to you and then memorize it together. Point out things that you can tell them God is responsible for, like a beautiful sunset. You can say, "Look at the beautiful sunset God made for us," or "Thank you, Lord, for all those pretty flowers we get to enjoy." When you hear thunder you can say, "The Lord made thunder to remind us how powerful He is." That might calm younger children's fears of storms.

There is nothing more powerful than a praying mom. I think that's one of the reasons I'm still here today. My mom prays for my brother and me every morning. As I look back at my adventurous life (and now as well), I definitely needed a praying mother. Recently, at a Christian conference, I learned how important a praying mother is, and I made a lifetime commitment to pray for my husband's children every single day. They have been through so much with the divorce and tough times in high school that I decided to commit myself to be their "praying mother." I make a point every morning to take time out of my schedule on their behalf and pray for their health and safety. I pray for them to have good judgment and make the right decisions and many other things as well.

If you have children, get together with two to three other moms once a week or once a month to pray together for each other's children. Share with your friends the needs and desires you have for your kids as they grow up in this fallen world. Wouldn't it be a privilege to pray for your children and your friends' children throughout life? Everyone needs a prayer team!

Think about a couple of friends you trust and can confide in. Ask them to meet with you and pray for all your children. Keep a journal of your requests and God's answers. Someday you will look back in awe and ask, "Can you believe how the Lord brought us through that problem, and that one, and that one?"

If someone is doing you or your child wrong, pray for that person. Then wait and see how the Lord is going to answer your prayer. Always pray for the Lord to put a "shield of protection" around your family and friends.

I have three friends who have committed to meet together once a month for prayer. Our requests are confidential, and we pray for our children throughout the month for specific things. It's a comfort to know that my step-children are being prayed for, not only by me and their dad, but three other praying moms as well. It has brought us closer as friends, and I look forward to seeing how the Lord will be working in the lives of our children.

When I met Ben, I was concerned about marrying someone with kids and how I would feel about having "step-children." I prayed about it long and hard. The Lord put them on my heart and gave me a love for those girls that I can't explain. This is just another example of a situation when I knew in my heart and mind it was God's doing. I could not love those girls as I do if the Lord had not put them on my heart. I'm crazy about them! I care for them and I want the best for them, as if they were my own. I'm so blessed to have two beautiful, sweet, smart, loving step-daughters. I could not ask for more.

Prayer Tips

Here are some helpful tips to remember about prayer:

Start your day with prayer.

Always ask the Father in the authority of Jesus' name.

Pray about everything; be specific.

It's our choice to pray. Even when you are discouraged, don't stop praying. God wants to hear from His children. Every time you pray, it strengthens your faith. So also remember to:

Pray consistently without giving up.

Pray persistently without growing weary.

Pray expectantly without losing heart.

In January of 2007, Sandy began a new series on the Holy Spirit and taught the class one of my favorite prayers yet. I've prayed it every day since, and it has been most rewarding. It goes something like this:

"Lord, this is Your day and Your body. I'm available for You to lead me today. Block me if I start to go the wrong way. I want to be controlled by the Holy Spirit. Please guide me and show me Your will. I'm available to You."

Here are some other good prayers I've learned over the years with Sandy:

"Lord, please show me Your will for my life. Give me the desire to do Your will."

"Lord, the Creator of the universe who can do all things, I ask for Your peace and comfort as I go through this trial. Open my eyes to see what it is that you are teaching me. I know that You will sustain me. Thank You."

"Dear Jesus, thank You for dying on the cross for my sins so that I may spend eternity in heaven with You."

"Father, help me to focus on You, not on my situation. Remind me that all things happen according to Your purpose and by Your permission."

"And we know that in all things God works for the good of those who love Him."

"Dear Lord and Savior, please put a shield of protection around my family and friends."

Here are some other prayers I pray daily:

"Precious Father, help me to comply and submit to Your agenda, not mine. Block my way when I begin to get caught up in doing my agenda. Open my eyes, ears and heart to what You want me to do, so I don't miss any opportunities You may have waiting for me."

"Lord, please allow and encourage me to spend more time with You in prayer. Search me, O God, and know my heart. Allow me to see the things in my life that need to be changed. Conform me to be more like You."

"I ask You, Lord, to remove any self-centeredness and reorient me towards You so that I'm available to do Your work."

"Lord, remind me that when I'm suffering there is a lesson to be learned. Do not let me miss the lesson You are trying to teach me."

"I ask You, Lord, to please free me of any sin in my life that could be hindering my relationship with You. Allow me to recognize it and get rid of it."

"Lord, allow me to be able to forgive others and pray for those who bother me and persecute me."

"Please, Lord, don't let me get distracted by the devil or be too busy when You send someone to me. Open my eyes to see who You are putting in my path and how I can help them."

"Allow me to humble myself so that You don't have to do it for me. Enable me and use me to complete the tasks You give me."

"Thank You for my family and friends. I pray that You would bless them and their families. Lord, please bless the ones that pray for me. Allow them to feel Your peace."

"Thank You, Lord, for blessing me. I praise Your name and I ask that I will always glorify You and give You the credit You deserve."

"Lord, I want to thank You for going before me, walking alongside me and behind me. Thank You for protecting me, even when I don't realize it. Thank You for always being there for me, to guide me and protect me. You are faithful and worthy. I praise Your name."

"Dear Lord, please don't allow me to be conformed to the rest of the world. Help me be a

person who will lead others to You by the way I live. Help me live and act in a way that will attract others to You. Please reveal Your purposes and Your will for my life today." That doesn't mean that I'm perfect or that I don't cause others to stumble. I am a work in progress, and will be the rest of my life.

One of my greatest hopes is that this book will help you understand the importance of prayer and having an intimate relationship with the Lord. People don't realize the power of prayer, but the Lord tells us all through Scripture how important it is and that He answers our prayers.

"Wait for the Lord and keep his way. He will exalt you to inherit the land; when the wicked are cut off, you will see it."
Psalm 37:34

"God is our refuge and strength, an ever-present help in trouble. Therefore we will not fear..."
Psalm 46:1–2

"Be still and know that I am God."
Psalm 46:10

Chapter 8

Sharing Your Faith

You don't have to have a degree in ministry to share your faith. You can plant little seeds in people without having to perform a sermon. Just mentioning the church you attend or that you are part of a Bible class can open up a conversation with someone who is lost or reaching for an answer. The answer is Christ!

As Christians, we need to be aware of what is going on around us. God gives us opportunities to share our faith every day. Be on the lookout for opportunities that might be around you. You might be friends with someone who doesn't know Christ. Your life might just be the only Bible that he or she will ever read. You might be the only person who mentions the Bible, church or Jesus to them. Don't waste an opportunity to share the Good News of Jesus with someone. Another prayer Sandy taught me is:

"Lord, if it's Your will, let me speak of You today."

One of my favorite places to witness to people is on an airplane. You have just enough time to plant seeds (or even more), plus they can't get away! A lot of times when I'm flying by myself I read my Bible or I do my lessons for Bible class. Several times, the person next to me will ask, "What are you studying?" To me, that's my cue to plant a seed or do whatever the Lord leads me to do.

After I say what I'm studying, that usually opens up the conversation. I always stick to the fact that what the Bible teaches is truth. If they ask questions, I try to be as clear as I can when answering them. That's another good reason to know Scripture. John 3:16 is a great verse for witnessing because it says, *"For God so loved the world that he gave his one and only Son, that whoever believes in him shall not perish but have eternal life."* I learned that verse in church when I was about five years old. It's been in my mind ever since, and it is easy to remember.

When you are sharing your faith with someone, you need to have a three-minute (short version) and five-minute (more detailed version) of your testimony. Your testimony is your story about how you became a Christian and how the Lord has changed you or helped you in a time of crisis. It helps to write it out and practice it every once in a while. That way, if you have an opportunity to share your story, you can tell it with confidence and not fumble around for words.

When people hear a "firsthand" story, it makes a much greater impact on them, rather than telling a story about another person (especially if they don't know you or the other person). The most convincing stories are those that tell how the Lord worked in your life and describe how the result was more than you expected because you trusted God.

Ministering in Prison

An example of a story I might share with someone is about the first time I went to prison. God used me in a way I never thought could happen. As part of a ministry to prisoners, my church placed white paper bags out front one Sunday for anyone to take home and decorate. You could draw crosses, Bible verses or whatever you wanted pertaining to Jesus. A ministry called Cornerstone Ministries from Wyllie, Texas would then fill the bags with soap, shampoos, deodorant and fruit and give them as "blessing bags" at a women's prison.

I brought a couple of bags home with me and decorated them. I had no idea what the Lord was about to do in my life, but I decided to donate money to help them buy items that would go in the bags. Over the next week, I started to think about going with the mission group to deliver the blessing bags. They were scheduled to go the Sunday before Christmas. As a photographer, leaving the studio in December is crazy. Everybody wants their Christmas cards yesterday, even if they placed their order yesterday! Even so, the thought kept coming to my mind about going to the prison.

I called the chaplain in charge and asked some questions about the program. When he told me we would be leaving at five in the morning on Sunday, that about killed it for me. However, after a couple more days passed, the time was becoming less of an obstacle. I couldn't stop thinking about going to the prison and witnessing to the ladies. Finally, I called the chaplain back and told him I'd like to join them on their journey to Gatesville, Texas to deliver the blessing bags. It was still a couple of weeks away, but as the date approached I grew even more excited.

Then the night before the trip, I felt Satan working on me. All of a sudden, I didn't want to get up at four in the morning to be ready to leave at five. It was a three-hour drive and I hate driving. I didn't know anyone going except one guy I met years ago in a Bible class.

So, I called the chaplain about seven that night, looking for a way out. His wife answered with a friendly, "Hello."

"Ah, yes... my name is Amy and I am supposed to go with ya'll tomorrow..." I said as I began preparing my excuse.

"Yes, Amy, we are very excited to meet you."

"Oh, great," I thought to myself. I decided to ask her a question and buy more time. "Are we going to be able to witness to the girls in their cells?"

"Oh no, Sugar," she replied sweetly. "All we do is pass out the blessing bags. We don't talk to the girls at all. We just tell them, 'Jesus loves you' as we pass out the bags."

I couldn't muster up the nerve to make my excuse so I just said, "Oh, okay. Well, see you in the morning," and hung up the phone. Now, not only did I have to get up before dawn, I wouldn't even get to witness to the girls!

I stewed for a moment and thought, "Satan is trying to talk me out of this." I brushed off the last of my excuses and decided, "At least I'll get to go and see what it's all about." Four o'clock came earlier than I expected. (What did I expect? It's in the middle of the night!) I met the rest of the team (about 13 people total) and we left as planned from the church parking lot at five on the dot. It was a long drive in the dark, and we arrived at the Murry Unit in Gatesville at eight. The temperature was in the low 40s and chilly.

The Murry Unit is a maximum security prison. I had never been to a prison before and noted that everyone is so serious. (I, on the other hand, am not.) We went through several security gates, the kind that lock behind you and in front of you to let you into the cage of locked doors. Our goal was to give each girl in the prison a blessing bag as they exited the mess hall.

We stood out there for about thee hours passing out the bags. We were instructed to say, "Jesus loves you—this is a blessing from the Lord." But I thought that sounded a little "cultish." Not realizing it mattered too much, I began saying "Merry Christmas, God bless you!" instead. One of the male team members leaned in between me and one of the four girls I was standing with and reprimanded me. He said, "You can't say 'God bless you' because there are many gods. You need to say 'Jesus loves you.'" Then he added, "And don't say 'Merry Christmas' either because there are girls with different faiths and we don't want to offend them."

After he went back to his job of stacking the bags, I turned to the girl next to me and whispered, "Who's the drill sergeant?"

The girl responded slowly, "He is my husband."

Ever say something and then wish you could take it back and no one would remember? That was one of many of those times for me. The other girls helping with me giggled under their breath, so I didn't feel too bad.

Two prisoners were allowed to help us, Mary and Falishia. After three hours, we'd become friends and we were cutting up and having fun. While we were waiting for the next group of girls, I noticed an older Hispanic lady in cuffs walking between two big armed guards. I half-jokingly asked Mary, "Why are they guarding that elderly lady? It's not like she's gonna outrun them."

She said, "You don't recognize her? That's the lady that killed Selena (the young Latino singer). They guard her so that the other prisoners won't kill her." All of the sudden, I became serious. That really got my attention. I had followed all the media stories that aired about how Selena had been murdered by the woman who managed her fan club. After Mary said that, I did recognize her. She looked much older than on television.

Then I began wondering what Mary did to end up in prison. I never asked; it wasn't my business. If she wanted me to know, she would tell me. About 15 minutes passed and Mary said to me, "Amy, will you pray for me?" I told her, "Of course I will." She continued, "I'm up for parole in six months...I've been here 19 years." She didn't look old enough to be there 19 years. I told her I'd be glad to pray for her.

She went on, "My sentence is 45 years."

I'm sure the expression on my face changed, but I tried to act like it was not a big deal. I can only imagine what someone had to have done to earn a 45-year sentence. I guess I'll never know, not until I get to heaven anyway. I was happy when she also told me she had accepted Christ while in prison and He had changed her life. I believe I was there in that prison that day to encourage her and let her know someone was praying for her. I even wrote her a couple of letters and sent her some books to read.

If you have not read the *Purpose Driven Life*, I can tell you from my experience that it can change your life. It changed mine in a wonderful way and I encourage you to read it. If you have already read it, read it again. The second time I read this book, I was at a different place in my life than the first time. I gained a different perspective on it the second time around.

It was because of that book that I got more involved with helping others. Between Sandy's lessons, reading that book and the Holy Spirit molding me, I've come so far in my spiritual journey. I have a hunger for the Lord that I've never before experienced. I crave my "quiet time" with Him each morning. I've recognized that no matter what happens in my life or to those around me, the Lord allowed it to happen for a reason. He is always working behind the scenes for our good. Sometimes it seems hard, but we eventually see God's plan if we have open eyes and hearts for the Lord to reveal it to us. A great example is my dad's death. I could sit around all day asking, "Why, Lord? Why my Dad? He was a strong Christian and lived the Christian life, why him?" Now I realize that it was my dad's death that began my spiritual journey. The Lord called him home and, because of that, I began a new life.

God Rewards You for Serving and Sharing

Hebrews 6:9–12 says, *"...we are confident of better things in your case—things that accompany salvation. God is not unjust, he will not forget your work and the love you have shown him as you have helped his people and continue to help them. We want each of you to show this same diligence to the very end, in order to make your hope sure. We do not want you to become lazy, but to imitate those who through faith and patience inherit what has been promised."*

How encouraging to know that God will not forget or overlook the things we do through Him. He has asked us to treat others as we would treat ourselves. When we help others, through volunteer work or in the church, God will reward us. We have hope that keeps us from becoming lazy or bored if we know that the Lord appreciates and will not forget the good things we've done. You can't imitate what you don't know. But now that you know what God wants us to do, you have no excuses for not sharing your faith and helping others. Knowledge without application is a waste of time. Be willing and available to Him for His use.

Some Christians are great at volunteering, helping others and donating their time. However, it is possible to be a Christian and not let the Holy Spirit lead or control you. Some Christians are led by the flesh, but not by the Spirit. That means they follow their human desires—doing things to make themselves look good and bragging that they have "volunteered their time" at a homeless shelter. This behavior focuses on self rather than on actions that would please the Lord. They do not have the knowledge that "this is what the Lord desires." If you don't have any desire to help others, ask the Lord to give you a desire so that your willingness to help is real, not just because you want a reward from God.

It's an ongoing battle to live the Christian life. Satan is always there to make worldly things more attractive to us and distract us from doing the right thing. First Peter 5:8–11 says, *"Be self-controlled and alert. Your enemy the devil prowls around like a roaring lion looking for someone to devour. Resist him, standing firm in the faith, because you know that your brothers throughout the world are undergoing the same kind of sufferings. And the God of all grace, who called you to his eternal glory in Christ, after you have suffered a little while, will himself restore you and make you strong, firm and steadfast. To him be the power for ever and ever. Amen."*

God asks us to walk in faith, but He doesn't ask us to do it alone. Jesus has a plan and a will for you. God has already planned your life and decided your spiritual gifts. Desire the Lord's will for you! Let God show you where and how to go. He is your ability, so you must trust Him to work in you. Trusting in Him doesn't mean your life will be smooth and perfect with no problems, but you will have the support of the Creator of the universe.

Make the choice. The plan is His. As believers, we have access by faith to Christ, who is always sufficient and available to us. Remember, we were designed to be inadequate in ourselves and to be dependent on Christ. We have to trust Him to be our sufficiency, and when we do, He will enable us to function beyond our human ability. He asks us to have faith in Him, and He promises to help us be confident that we don't have to live our lives alone. He is all you will ever need in any situation you'll ever have. In our darkest hours we fully discover who He is.

God Enables You to Share Your Faith in Trials

When some people think of sharing their faith, they get hung up on practicing religion a certain way or attending a certain church. It's not which church you go to, but your personal relationship with Christ that matters most. However, if you can go to a church that is Scripture-based it will help you to grow in your faith. We all need to put our hope, trust and faith in Christ as our Savior. No single church alone can save us, meet our needs or give us hope. Hope comes from Christ living in us.

I find that when my friends are faced with difficult situations, they call and ask me to pray for them. This also opens a door for me to give them Bible verses that relate to their particular situation. They are much more open to hear what the Bible says during difficult times. I reassure them that if they turn their problems over to the Lord, He will give them peace in the midst of their trials if they will trust Him.

God will enable us to share our faith. If you feel that someone is reaching out or asking a question about God or faith in God, stop and pray silently, even while the person is talking. For example, you might pray:

"Lord, put the words in my mouth. Please speak through me, and let Sarah's heart be open to hear

what you are saying through me. Use me, Lord, to help her understand and comprehend what she is confused about."

As we live our lives, we experience many trials. We need to realize that the Lord puts trials in our lives so that we will depend on Him to get through them. There is a lesson to be learned from each difficulty we endure. Let the Lord take control. Then sit back and watch to see how He will work in your life. Doing this is beneficial to you and those around you. The people who surround you will see that the Lord is glorified in you, and hopefully they will be attracted to God. We are God's advertisement!

On many occasions, Sandy has told me how important it is to be strong in your faith. Sharing your faith can be with words, but also with actions. Sandy has always been a glowing illustration of someone who walks the walk. By being with her, I can feel a sense of peace, grace and love. Sandy and I laugh from time to time when I tell her that someday she will be magna cum laude in heaven and will probably have a chair next to Jesus' throne! She has always been so humble, but those who know her believe that she probably will be next to Him!

God tells us who He is through Scripture, so we must be willing to trust and apply what we know about Him to our lives. Needs give us the opportunity to do that. When He gives us a need, and then fulfills it after we pray and ask for help, He proves to us that He is there, He cares, He is reality and He is trustworthy.

Needs are the fertilizer for spiritual growth. Paul tells us we can have peace through faith during our trials. In fact, the trials serve to strengthen our faith. The more trials we endure, the greater our faith becomes. It's easy to have great faith if everything is going our way and we don't have any needs, but trials and testing build our faith, making it strong and real.

Sandy offered a strengthening prayer for those times when we're faced with difficulty and feel like we're alone:

"Lord, I will wait for You. I believe in You. I know You have a plan. I know You exist, and I know You love me. I'll wait for You in this trial to give me peace that surpasses all understanding. Lord, Your ability to meet my needs is far beyond what I can imagine."

If you feel He is not responding, read Scripture so He can speak to you through His Word. Pray before You read:

"Lord, I'm Your child. I need to hear from You!"

My friend, Melissa, was recently in the middle of the biggest crisis of her life. She was married for 15 years to a man who was unfaithful with her friend. While she was looking for a job, her father suffered a heart attack, and her mentally-challenged brother lost his temper and tried to hurt his caregiver. She flew back home to help her father and brother. When she arrived, she learned that her mom had developed congenital heart failure and needed to have a pacemaker. All of these events happened within two weeks. Can you say, "Crisis"? Calamity? Major trial and testing?

Yet the first time I talked to her, she told me she felt the Lord's peace. She felt His comfort and knew that He was in control. Her story is an outstanding example of faith, trust and belief that what God says about giving us peace during trials is true! She also told me she and her mom could feel the prayers lifting them up and encouraging them. (I e-mailed my prayer warriors to ask that everyone pray for her and her family.)

Melissa and I are in a small Bible class on Tuesday nights. We have been studying a workbook called "Experiencing God," by Henry Blackaby. I believe that through this workbook, the Lord has been preparing Melissa for this time in her life. I believe God has given her the grace with which she is handling all of this. What a privilege it is that God gives us the faith we need in order to experience His peace through the toughest times in our life. Trust your problems to the Lord, and He will give you His supernatural peace and permeate your soul with an indescribable peace that only He can give. That's what the Christian life offers. It's the "unshakable faith" that Sandy describes.

When something tragic happens, we must refocus. God is sufficient. Remember that He allows problems to occur in order that we might come to Him and ask for help. When He gives us the help or an answer, we give Him the glory. There are no accidents as far as God is concerned, and He is adequate for every situation. James 1:2–3 says, *"Consider it pure joy, my brothers, whenever you face trials of many kinds, because you know that the testing of your faith develops perseverance."* In other words, ask God to change you, not the situation. There is a reason for the things God allows to happen in our lives. One reason may be to open your eyes so that you may change your ways.

Share Your Faith in Several Ways

There are many ways to share our faith. There are the obvious ways, such as being a missionary or a pastor, but not everyone is created to be a minister. You can plant seeds by inserting certain phrases into your daily conversations, such as "The Lord blessed me when He …" or "I'd love to play golf on Sunday, but we'd need to go after church." If you hear someone in the family is sick, you can say, "I'm so sorry to hear about that. What's his/her name? I'll pray for them." Or if you know people going through a tough time, read some verses to them or write them a note that includes a verse about God's peace, comfort or encouragement.

Here are a few verses to get you started:

The Lord is my rock, my fortress and my deliverer; my God is my rock, in whom I take refuge. He is my shield and the horn of my salvation, my stronghold.
—Psalm 18:2

Cast your cares on the Lord and he will sustain you; he will never let the righteous fall.
—Psalm 55:22

I call on the Lord, who is worthy of my praise, and I am saved from my enemies.
—Psalm 18:3

Call upon me in the day of trouble; I will deliver you, and you will honor me.
—Psalm 50:15

Praise be to the God and Father of our Lord Jesus Christ, the Father of compassion and the God of all comfort, who comforts us in all our troubles, so that we can comfort those in any trouble with the comfort we ourselves have received from God.
—2 Corinthians 1:3–4

Remember that when you have a hardship above your ability to handle, you qualify for God's all-surpassing power. Expect His peace and comfort to kick in and provide you with the power and strength you need.

Romans 8:18 says, *"I consider that our present sufferings are not worth comparing with the glory that will be revealed in us."* This verse gives me hope and assurance that all my problems will be nothing when God's glory is revealed in us. We will wonder why we ever lost sleep over certain things. (That doesn't mean that I sleep peacefully every night!)

God is not working to make us happy; He is fulfilling His purpose. His purpose is only for those who love God and have accepted Him as their Savior. It is for those who look for their security in heaven, not treasures here on earth. They learn to accept trials and not be resentful of them. Second Corinthians 4:17–18 is one of my favorite Scriptures: *"For our light and momentary troubles are achieving for us an eternal glory that far outweighs them all. So we fix our eyes not on what is seen, but on what is unseen. For what is seen is temporary, but what is unseen is eternal.*" As these verses explain, nothing we go through here on earth is worth worrying about. Focus on God and heaven, and your troubles will seem small and insignificant.

Second Corinthians 12:9–10 reminds us, "'...*My grace is sufficient for you, for my power is made perfect in weakness'...for when I am weak, then I am strong.*" The fact that God's power is displayed in weak people should encourage us. Remember what God did through Moses, Abraham, David, Paul and many others.

John 16:33 says, *"In this world you will have trouble. But take heart! I have overcome the world."* God tells us, "In me you will have peace." He doesn't say, "Except when ..." His word is truth and we can be assured that what He says, He means.

Romans 5:2–5 is another good passage that says, *"And we rejoice in the hope of the glory of God. Not only so, but we also rejoice in our sufferings, because we know that suffering produces perseverance; perseverance, character; and character, hope. And hope does not disappoint us, because God has poured out his love into our hearts by the Holy Spirit, whom he has given us."* We get to enjoy the peace that God gives us when we are right with Him, but we still have daily problems that help us grow in our faith.

As we endure problems throughout our lives, we will learn to depend on the love, peace and power that are available to us through Christ and the Holy Spirit that lives within us. As Philippians 4:13 says, *"I can do everything through him who gives me strength."* Instead of worrying or stressing over work, home or school, pray about it!

Don't be embarrassed or scared to stand up for what you believe. You never know whose life will become "eternal" because you planted a seed, no matter how nonchalant your comment may seem. *"Whoever acknowledges me before man, I will also acknowledge him before my Father in heaven,"* Matthew 10:32. It's important to remember that we have a limited time on earth to share our faith with other people. We don't know when Jesus is going to return. We don't know when we're going to die or our friends and family are going to die. One day, it may be too late to share your faith, and you will wish you had.

"...I tell you the truth, whatever you did for one of the least of these brothers of mine, you did for me."
Matthew 25:40

"Always be prepared to give an answer to everyone who asks you to give the reason for the hope that you have."
1 Peter 3:15

Chapter 9

What Is Your Story?

Whenever Sandy's Bible classes start back up after our Christmas break, I am always eager to begin again. I look forward to finding out what the New Year's lesson is going to be about. I've had to miss several Bible classes over the years because my tennis matches fall on Thursday mornings. (Unfortunately I got injured last season, but that means I can make all of Sandy's classes this year! Who says God doesn't have a sense of humor?)

Sandy starts the class off by introducing any women who are visiting for the first time. Recently, I brought six people with me, and when I raised my hand to introduce everyone, Sandy remarked, "My goodness! Amy has the whole row!" I was so excited my friends came with me to class, and I was anxious for them to meet Sandy because I always talked about her.

Several people had asked Sandy, "Teach us more on the Second Coming!" So Sandy agreed to start the first class that year on the tribulation and Second Coming of Christ. I've always been so intrigued with the "End Times." Since I was about 15 years old, I have had very vivid dreams. I sometimes call them "visions" because they are so real to me that I can feel it, hear it and experience it.

Dreaming about the Rapture

In one dream, I was in a field. The grass was very green as if it were the beginning of springtime. There were rolling hills without any trees all around me. I could see forever, and it was so pretty. I was standing with a friend that I had known since childhood. She was wearing a white sundress with little red flowers on it. All of the sudden, the loudest surround sound of trumpets shook the earth. It wasn't a disturbing loud sound (like a teenager's sub-woofer at a traffic light); it was beautiful, and it was everywhere. The clouds began to part and the sky grew bright, but not from the sun. It just became super bright everywhere. As I looked around, I noticed thousands of people including myself slowly ascending towards heaven. I could hear singing now, and I know without a doubt it was the voices of angels. I was experiencing the Rapture.

In my dream, I glanced around at the thousands of people floating towards heaven and I felt a peace and a joy in my heart like I'd never felt before. I looked back at my friend and then she, too, was ascending into heaven. It was by far the most vivid, powerful vision I'd ever had until my dad passed away.

I had two other vivid and real dreams that were similar to that one about the Rapture. My parents and

I have a longstanding joke where I tell them, "I pray for the Rapture to come so we can all go together, and I forbid you to die before me." We all laugh when we talk about it, but the truth is that I can't imagine life without Mom and Harold. They are such a strong and steady foundation in my life.

Heaven Is a Happy Reunion

After college and I moved to Maui, I was only there about four weeks when I got the call from my mom that my grandmother had died. "Grandmoma" (my mother's mother) was my favorite of my four grandparents. She was funny, had a great sense of humor and always spoke her mind.

I remember my mom often saying, "Oh, mother" whenever Grandmoma would say something off color. She was queen of the "Eastern Star," a women's organization in Tyler, Texas. She was very admired and involved in her community. One of my favorite stories about her took place when she and my grandfather, Harry, were fishing at a private lake in Tyler. They were in a small, aluminum boat on a Saturday afternoon enjoying the day when suddenly a ski boat full of teenagers zoomed by way too close, rocking their little boat with their wake. Grandmoma and Harry held tightly to the sides until the water settled, only to see the boat circling back a few minutes later, this time with a skier in tow.

The teenagers once again came roaring past their small fishing boat as they held tight and prepared to ride out the wake. However, they were not expecting what happened next. The skier skidded across the water and sprayed Grandmoma and Harry from head to toe. All the kids just laughed as Grandmoma and Harry clung to the nearly swamped boat and water dripped off their hats. That was the icing on the cake for Grandmoma.

The boat was turning around to make another pass at them when Grandmoma got an idea. She reached down and grabbed a paddle from the bow of the boat. Harry knew better than to try to stop her. I don't think he had any idea what she was going to do with the paddle, and neither did the skier. The young girl was laughing and joking with her friends as she skied right over to my grandparents' boat to spray them again. At just the precise moment, Grandmoma launched the paddle at the girl, who suddenly wasn't laughing anymore. Nobody messes with my Grandmoma! I give her the credit for all my spunk.

When Mom called, I burst into tears. I hated that I wasn't there. Not only that, I had a 12-hour flight ahead of me. I cried the entire way, and it was the longest flight I can remember. Two months after Grandmoma went to be with the Lord, I had an unusual dream in a way I had never before experienced. The dream about the Rapture was really neat, and it was exciting to me to think about how close that dream will be to what will eventually happen. However, this dream was even more vivid than the other one. For the first time, my dream had crossed over to reality. I remember it like it was yesterday.

I woke up crying so hard I couldn't catch my breath. It was dark outside as I glanced at the clock. It was 5:00 a.m. in Maui. I calculated quickly and determined it was 11:00 in the morning, Dallas time. I rolled over, picked up the phone and called my mom. I was trying to catch my breath, still in tears. "Mom," I cried into the phone, "I just saw Grandmoma."

"What?" Mom asked. She was confused.

"I just saw Grandmoma. She told me she was doing great and wasn't in any pain…they were taking great care of her and she was in a beautiful place. She told me she is fine…she is okay." With that, Mom began to cry, too. I started from the beginning and told her about my dream.

In it, I was in the back of a limo in front of the house where I grew up during my early years. Harry was with me, and we were talking. All of a sudden, it was as though a whirlwind entered the car. I looked over and Grandmoma was sitting beside me! We hugged each other so tightly that I could actually feel her embrace. I began to cry as I told her how much I missed her. "Oh, Grandmoma," I told her, "I miss you so much. Please come back…I love you so much.

Grandmoma said, "Honey, I am in a beautiful place. They are taking such good care of me. I don't have any pain. I feel good, and Harry is with me." My crying was so full of emotion and I kept repeating to myself, "Grandmoma, I miss you so much."

As we sat there looking at each other, she began to fade away. My crying grew more intense the more she began to disappear. That's when I woke up—crying so hard that I'd lost my breath. I can't describe the feeling exactly, but I felt her hugging me. I spoke to her. She spoke to me. And I had to wonder, "Is she really gone?" I felt as if God had given me a chance to say good-bye and that He was reassuring me she was in heaven and everything was okay.

We need to share the Gospel with as many people as possible so that they will have a chance to spend eternity in heaven with Jesus. If you and your loved ones have received Jesus as Savior and Lord, then you can be sure you will have a happy reunion with them one day in heaven. I was reminded of this important truth when I was on a trip to Russia to serve in a Russian orphanage. I met a special little girl in the orphanage who had blue eyes and a beautiful smile. We grew quite attached to one another during that time. My heart broke when she gave me the stuffed animal that she slept with every night as a reminder of her. When I was leaving, she looked up at me with her blue eyes full of concern and asked, "Will I see you again?" I assured her that what she had heard in Bible class was true. If she received Jesus into her life, then one day she would see me again. We would have a happy reunion in heaven.

Remember this story the next time that you part from someone you love and he or she asks you, "When will I see you again?" It could lead into the perfect opportunity to share your faith with that person. Be on the lookout to share your faith in your everyday life—the opportunities are all around you. Sometimes you can be a witness to someone else without even knowing it.

Share Your Faith in Everyday Ways

One day I called Sandy to ask her if I could come over to catch up. I see her at Bible class every week, but we don't have a chance to chat. I asked her to tell me the story about her neighbor who lived behind her in Tulsa, Oklahoma where she and her husband, Red, lived before they moved to Dallas in 1959. Her story is a good example of how sharing even one sentence pertaining to Christ can plant seeds in those around you.

Sandy and "Nancy" had kids the same age, and they enjoyed the friendship that had formed between them. One day Red came home after a breakfast meeting with his boss and told Sandy, "My boss asked if we'd like to move to Dallas. Would you like to?" Although Sandy and Red were raised in Dallas, they both loved Tulsa and were not too keen on moving. They had a new house and had made many friends. Even so, they agreed to pray about it over the next week while Red was out of town. Sandy recalls, "We knew that God has a will, and His will has a geographical location. If Dallas was where God wanted us, we both agreed that it was His choice, not ours." During the next week, they both prayed and asked the Lord what He would have them do.

When Red returned on Friday, he and Sandy discussed the option of moving. Red asked, "How are you feeling about moving to Dallas?"

"I feel like the Lord wants us to go," Sandy said simply.

Red confirmed her feelings and replied, "I think He does, too."

So, they agreed that the Lord was leading them to Dallas for reasons they didn't yet know. They accepted the job, following the instinct God had given them, and began the process of moving. At the time, three oil companies had been decentralized, and people were moving out of Tulsa by the hundreds. There were so many homes up for sale—at least four or five on Sandy's block alone—and it was not a sellers market, to say the least.

The first assurance that this was what God wanted them to do came through a friend who told her one day, "I have a friend who wants to come with me for our Bible class on Tuesday." It was Sandy's turn to host a women's Bible class at her house, and she said that her friend's guest was welcome to come. As ladies often do, her friend asked Sandy if she could give her guest a tour of Sandy's new home.

Sandy was happy to let her look, not really thinking anything of it. In a few moments, the lady that looked at her house returned and said, "Sandy, I love your house." Sandy made the casual, off-handed remark, "Well, it's available." Sandy and Red had not even listed the house with a realtor yet, and the woman certainly wasn't looking to buy a home. "Oh no," she said. "We're not in the market."

However, the phone was ringing later that night just as Sandy and Red were walking into their house after being out. Sandy picked up the phone and it was that same woman.

She said, "Sandy, my husband and I drove by your home earlier this afternoon. Would you mind if he came with me to see the inside again?"

"Of course not," Sandy said.

Guess who bought Sandy's house? Not only did they buy it, but they paid the asking price in cash! It couldn't have happened in an easier or quicker way, which let them know that this was a God thing. Sandy recalls, "We got every penny we were asking for. Sometimes God does things in such an amazing way that you just have to know it was His doing." Their feelings and prayers had been confirmed, and they were on their way to Dallas. But God was not through with this story yet.

When Nancy heard at a school meeting that Sandy was moving, she came by her house. It was not easy telling her friend, whom she loved and adored, why they were moving. You see, Nancy was an atheist. She and her husband had been involved with a group in college that had persuaded them in that direction. Whenever Sandy would mention "the Lord," Nancy would roll her eyes in her gentle way. She couldn't possibly understand that the "Lord" had led them to Dallas.

They were sitting on the sofa in Sandy's living room when Nancy said, "Sandy, I'm crushed that you have to move to Dallas."

Sandy explained, "It isn't that we *have* to leave, but we've prayed about it and we believe it's God's will for us to go." Sandy thought at the time, *Why am I saying this? This is sailing right over her head.* However, that was the way she said it and a little while later, Sandy and Red moved to Dallas in October of 1959.

The following Christmas, Sandy received a Christmas card from Nancy. At the bottom of the card, Nancy had written, "When you're back in Tulsa, come by because I have something to share with you."

The next spring, Red went back to Tulsa on business, and Sandy went to visit her old friend. As she walked into the entryway of her house, Nancy smiled and said, "Oh, Sandy, I know your precious Lord and Savior."

Sandy was overwhelmed. Both ladies had tears welling up in their eyes and Sandy asked, "Oh, how did this happen?"

Just as Nancy was about to begin telling Sandy the story, her husband rounded the corner. When Bill came in, Sandy remembered where he stood in his beliefs and thought, *Well, this ends that conversation.* However, times had changed.

"Hi Sandy," he greeted her and asked, "Where do you go to church in Dallas?"

She told him and then to Sandy's surprise and delight, Bill named her pastor. "How did you know that?" Sandy asked.

"Well, I'm reading his book." Sandy let that thought sink in for a moment and exclaimed, "Bill, you too?"

"Didn't Nancy tell you?"

"No, we just started talking when you came in."

Bill continued, "Do you remember saying to Nancy when you were moving to Dallas that you didn't have to move, but you had prayed about it and you felt this was God's will for you?"

"Yes."

"Nancy came home and told me that, and I thought that was the most 'way out there' stuff I'd ever heard in my life...but it started a hunger in my heart. I wanted somebody that knew how to guide my life like that." Bill shared that not too long afterwards, a Christian businessman witnessed to him and he accepted Christ!

Nancy and Bill had come to trust in Christ, and the key factor was Sandy and Red's obedience to the Lord when they moved to Dallas. They trusted Christ to guide them and shared that trust with Nancy. That one comment from Sandy (prompted by the Lord) planted a seed, launching her friends into a life with Christ. In fact, all three of Nancy and Bill's children are involved in the ministry—both daughters married men in Christian work, and their son is a pastor.

As Sandy looked back at what happened, she made a point to tell me, "It's so important to always be obedient to the Lord because we never know what we would miss by being disobedient." She and Red could easily have told the Lord, "We don't want to move. We like it here. Our kids have their lives here, too." However, because they prayed about it and were open to following the Lord's will, many things have happened since they moved to Dallas. They know that God's way is perfect. Therefore, He makes our way perfect.

Everybody Needs a Sandy

Over the years, Sandy and Red have experienced many other confirmations that they did the right thing by following God's will for them. I'm so thankful that they did; otherwise, I wouldn't have met Sandy! By sharing her faith and knowledge with me, Sandy has been my mentor and changed my life in so many ways. Let me ask you, "Can you be a 'Sandy' to someone else?" Do you have a desire for God to use you to tell others what it means to live the Christian life? Or you may be someone who needs someone like Sandy to guide them. Have you asked God to bring a "Sandy" into your life?

As I look back over all the things I've learned from her, several of her words of wisdom keep re-surfacing. I've shared so much of what I have learned from her, but there is no way to tell you the full impact she has had on my life. What Sandy has taught me comes straight from Scripture, and she says it in a way that is easy to understand and makes the truth a reality in my life. I know this is why Sandy has been successful in reaching so many people.

One day several years ago, I met Sandy at Starbucks around three o'clock. I had spent a month in Aspen, Colorado, hiking, taking photographs and going through some changes. We sat at the table in the back where there are fewer distractions and less noise. She leaned in close as I began to tell her with excitement what I'd been doing all summer.

I could tell that the Lord was nudging me to do something. I spent lots of time being still and quiet, more than I had ever had in the past. (As a matter of fact, I don't ever remember being still and quiet.) A long time ago, I had started a notebook with verses that referred to comfort, encouragement and reassurance. While in Aspen, I went through all the notes I'd taken from the meetings at Starbucks with Sandy, her Bible classes and church sermons.

I organized all the verses and advice and filled my notebook with a number of topics, beginning with "Comfort Verses," followed by "Becoming a Christian," "Worry," "Faith," "Dating and Marriage," "Trials and Testing," "Prayer," "Healing," "Forgiveness," "Refusing to Believe" and "When Satan Attacks." After I had organized my notebook with all the wisdom and knowledge Sandy had given me, I thought to myself, "It's a shame that I'm the only one who will get to benefit from all her wisdom from the Bible and the experiences she's had." Then the Lord put the thought in my mind, "Write a book, then you can share it with thousands of people!"

Looking back now, I realize what the Lord was nudging me to do...write this book!

So that is how this book came about. I wanted to share with others what I've learned and experienced with God. This book's message is to explain God's desire for your life in a simple way with a touch of humor. More importantly, it explains that when you have Christ in your life, you have everything (Romans 8:32).

Because of Sandy's great devotion to the Lord, He has given her wisdom and knowledge about Scripture. She has been able to bring the Scriptures to life for me, and I wanted to pass along what I have learned. I have simplified pages and pages of notes in order to share the importance of putting Christ first in your life. These funny, true stories are examples to show how Christ works in and through us for His good. Writing this book has drawn me closer to the Lord because of all the time I spent with God while putting it together. There is a peace in my life that I know comes from God, and I give Him glory for allowing me to experience His peace.

Most everything I've learned and recorded in this book came from Sandy and going to her classes all these years, not to mention all of our coffees and lunches! It made me realize that God has a purpose for each of our lives and how important it is to share our stories. Everyone has a story to share. Everybody needs a Sandy.

"Therefore go and make disciples of all nations…"
Matthew 28:19

"…God has given us eternal life, and this life is in his Son. He who has the Son has life; he who does not have the Son of God does not have life."
1 John 5:11–12

Epilogue

How to Become a Christian

The first step to becoming a Christian is believing what the Bible says is true. That can lead to a life of joy that is unimaginable, a life that we cannot fully comprehend until we learn what the Lord has in store for us—when we decide to give it all to Him and let Him have control of our lives.

You become a believer when by faith you make a conscious decision to ask Jesus into your heart. You also confess with your mouth that Jesus is Lord, and you believe He died on the cross for you personally and rose again in three days. Romans 10:9 says, *"That if you confess with your mouth, 'Jesus is Lord,' and believe in your heart that God raised him from the dead, you will be saved."*

Believing there is a God and going to church does not mean you are a Christian and are going to heaven. You must believe that Jesus died on the cross for your sins and rose again three days later. You must receive Him into your life, trust Him, believe in Him and have faith in Him to become a Christian and a "believer." Truly believing in Him will ensure that you spend eternity with Him in heaven. Are you absolutely sure that you know you are going to heaven when you die? On what do you base your answer? Scripture? Something you heard on television or read in a magazine? I once heard a statement that put it very simply. It said, "No Jesus, No Peace. Know Jesus, Know Peace."

What to Do Once You Are a Christian

As a believer, you should desire a personal and intimate relationship with your Creator. (If you don't, pray about it). To build a closer relationship, you need to spend time in prayer. Surround yourself with other Christians. Find a home church that teaches the truth. Get involved in a Bible study. Read the Bible and apply what you learn.

As I prayed and studied my Bible, God continued to teach me about what He wants me to do with my life. Ephesians 2:10 says, *"For we are God's workmanship, created in Christ Jesus to do good works, which God prepared in advance for us to do."* That verse says that God created us and, in Christ, He wants us to do good works. That was His intention for us before we were even born! Philippians 2:13 says almost the same thing, *"...for it is God who works in you to will and to act according to his good purpose."* This verse promises us that God is at work in us and through us.

He doesn't expect us to do what He wants on our own strength or power. He created us to do good works, and He will work His good purpose through you! Second

Peter 1:3–4 reminds us that God gives us everything we need in order to do His will. *"...His divine power has already granted us everything pertaining to life and godliness...so that by them we might become partakers of His divine nature."* (New American Standard)

Once you receive Christ as Lord of your life, you must begin to follow Him and learn more about Him. A lot of people have the wrong mindset about what happens once they accept Christ. They say, "Well, I've done that...I can check it off my list." There is more to it than that! Once you've received Him, follow up by learning more about what God has intended for your life. Colossians 2:6–10 encourages us by saying, *"So then, just as you received Christ Jesus as Lord, continue to live in him, rooted and built up in him, strengthened in the faith as you were taught, and overflowing with thankfulness. See to it that no one takes you captive through hollow and deceptive philosophy, which depends on human tradition and the basic principles of this world rather than on Christ. For in Christ all the fullness of the Deity lives in bodily form, and you have been given fullness in Christ, who is the head over every power and authority."*

Let's break down these verses so they are easier to understand. First of all, it says that we all have a lot more to learn about Christ no matter how long we've been Christians. God has so much available to us, but if we don't learn about it (reading Scripture, learning from sermons and Bible study classes) how can we enjoy the benefits of all He has for us? We need to commit our lives and submit to Him. Reach out and learn about Him and why He died for you. Investigate what the Bible teaches us about Him, His life, His will, His purposes and about us.

The next part of that passage in Colossians warns us about *why* it's important to know Him. The more you know about Him, the harder it will be for others to fool you and "buy into" their gods or remedies that can "cure all your problems."

Look again at verse 9 in that passage. It says: *"In Christ all the fullness of the Deity lives in bodily form."* This means that all of God was in Christ's human body. When we have Christ, we have everything we need. Christ alone is the source, and He is all we need to be saved and have eternal life.

How to Grow as a Christian

A few passages later, Colossians 3:1–10 tells us what to do next. In summary, it says: *"Set your hearts on things above, not on earthly things...put to death, therefore, whatever belongs to your earthly nature: sexual immorality, impurity, lust, evil desires and greed, which is idolatry. Because of these, the wrath of God is coming...rid yourselves of all such things...put on the new self, which is being renewed in knowledge in the image of its Creator."*

Once you are saved, ask God to help you get rid of the things in your life that are hindering your relationship with Him. This is an ongoing process. Sandy once said, "We are never free from the possibility of sinning or from the temptation to sin, but by being under the Spirit's control we are kept from responding to it." Whenever you are in a situation where something or someone is tempting you, start praying that you will not be tempted. Ask someone to pray with you or for you. They don't have to know the details. God knows what's going on. It has helped me in the past to ask my Bible class or a close friend to pray for me about a certain situation without having to explain too much. It can be an "unspoken prayer request," but I've learned that you can never have too many people praying for you!

"Salvation is found in no one else, for there is no other name under heaven given to men by which we must be saved."
Acts 4:12

Printed in the United States
200246BV00006B/160-2025/A

9 781604 772937